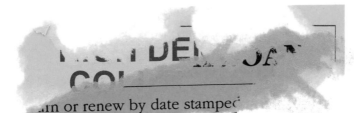

Research in the Classroom

TALK, TEXTS, AND INQUIRY

ZOE DONOAHUE

Lambton-Kingsway Junior Middle School, Etobicoke, Ontario

MARY ANN VAN TASSELL

The York School, Toronto, Ontario

LESLIE PATTERSON

University of Houston, Houston, Texas

EDITORS

INTERNATIONAL
Reading Association
800 BARKSDALE ROAD, PO BOX 8139
NEWARK, DE 19714-8139, USA

The International Reading Association attempts, through its publications, to provide a forum for a wide spectrum of opinions on reading. This policy permits divergent viewpoints without implying the endorsement of the Association.

Director of Publications   Joan M. Irwin
Assistant Director of Publications   Wendy Lapham Russ
Senior Editor   Christian A. Kempers
Associate Editor   Matthew W. Baker
Assistant Editor   Janet S. Parrack
Editorial Assistant   Cynthia C. Sawaya
Production Department Manager   Iona Sauscermen
Graphic Design Coordinator   Boni Nash
Design Consultant   Larry F. Husfelt
Desktop Publishing Supervisor   Wendy A. Mazur
Desktop Publisher   Anette Schütz-Ruff
Desktop Publisher   Cheryl J. Strum
Production Services Editor   David K. Roberts

Library of Congress Cataloging in Publication Data
    Research in the classroom: Talk, texts, and inquiry/Zoe Donoahue, Mary Ann Van Tassell, Leslie Patterson, editors.
        p.   cm.
    Includes bibliographical references and index.
    1. Action research in education—United States.   2. English language—Discourse analysis.
I. Donoahue, Zoe.   II. Van Tassell, Mary Ann.   III. Patterson, Leslie.
LB1028.24.R47   1996   96-4064
370'.78—dc20
ISBN 0-87207-146-4 (paper)

CONTENTS

Teachers as Researchers: Past and Present

Janice Lake Betts

Betts teaches courses in advanced reading, children's literature, and storytelling at Trenton State College in Trenton, New Jersey, USA. Her classes include teacher education students, experienced teachers and administrators, and general studies students, and are taught from an inquiry-based perspective that celebrates the role of arts in literacy. After focusing her doctoral research on playwriting with juvenile offenders, she continues to work with disadvantaged youth throughout the United States.

■ In 1993 the International Reading Association published *Teachers Are Researchers: Reflection and Action*, a project of the Teacher as Researcher Ad Hoc Committee. More than 100 articles were submitted in response to a call for manuscripts publicized throughout the United States, and the work of 25 teacher researchers was included in that volume, which was coedited by Leslie Patterson, Carol Minnick Santa, Kathy G. Short, and Karen Smith. Since this first publication milestone, the Teacher as Researcher committee has been working toward another volume to showcase the work of additional teacher researchers. It has also been a goal to involve public school teacher researchers in leadership roles in these publication projects.

This volume is one result of those efforts. It goes beyond offering an invitation to novice teacher researchers. It assembles the work of teacher researchers who are exploring the oral and written discourse of learning communities— communities of students, communities of teachers, and communities in which students and teachers learn together. The work of these teachers demonstrates that discourse is the both context and substance, product and process, of learning in these classrooms and campuses.

The range of research questions posed in this volume is impressive, with authors focusing on journal writing, conversation, storytelling, geometry, computer technology, and teacher collaboration. The common theme—the role of oral and written discourse within inquiry communities—is significant not only for these teachers, but for all literacy researchers. In Chapter 1, Leslie Patterson explores the common theoretical assumptions framing the work of these teachers, placing emphasis on the links among action, language, and thought. In Chapter 2, Marné Isakson and David Williams share their dialogue about what Marné learned from an analysis of her teaching journal. Chapter 3 focuses on Franca Fedele's work with elementary students as she encourages them to reflect on their learning. In Chapter 4, Judy Caulfield discusses how storytelling works for students in her classroom. Monica McGlynn-Stewart shifts our attention to the value of reflective talking and writing in an elementary math class in Chapter 5. In Chapter 6, Jeannine St. Pierre Hirtle adds an additional layer of complexity to the learning discourse within her high school classroom by using computers to collaborate across the curriculum. In Chapters 7 and 8, Zoe Donoahue and Flavia Churchill explore the power of collaborative inquiry among teacher communities. Finally, Marian Mohr offers an inspiring challenge to teacher researchers in her predictions for the future of teacher inquiry in Chapter 9.

These studies provide a lens through which all of us can learn more about how teacher researchers use discourse for their own inquiry and for finding ways to share their learning beyond their classrooms and campuses. With this volume, we invite you to join what Jerry Harste has called the "continuing conversation" about talk and texts within learning communities.

CHAPTER 1

Reliving the Learning: Learning From Classroom Talk and Texts

Leslie Patterson

After teaching and researching in middle and high schools for nine years, Patterson became a teacher educator and researcher. Since then she has written about teacher research and is currently working with preservice and inservice teachers at the University of Houston, Texas, USA, where her research focus is on collaborative inquiry in high school classrooms.

■ A few years ago I joined five colleagues to learn how to use portfolios in teacher education classes. We began what we called a "polylog," a notebook for collaborative reflection on our decisions and the students' responses. The polylog immediately enriched our teaching, learning, and friendships, but the most powerful learning came several months later, as we sat together to analyze those written conversations from each person's perspective. Through that collaborative analysis and reflection, we relived our moments of decision, indecision, confusion and discovery, and we realized the power of group inquiry when it is grounded in spoken and written discourse. The polylog was the source of our reflections, which we could access again and again. It was a record of our collective reflections and provided us with a foothold for our continuing inquiry.

Many teacher researchers are using the texts and the talk from their classrooms to participate in reflective discourse. They know that learning moments are captured in the classroom, and, through discourse teachers and their students can re-see and re-search those significant moments. Teachers invite their students to join the inquiry, to use a range of tools—journals, discussions, and storytelling—and to explore and question the world around them. These teachers encourage their students to revisit texts for new insights and new questions.

What can we learn from these teachers? We can learn that discourse is a medium for inquiry and that through discourse, people working together help one another learn. But exactly what does that mean? How does it happen? What can teacher researchers do to optimize the learning potential of both themselves and their students? In exploring answers to those questions, we see that a common view of learning frames the work of many teacher researchers.

Viewing Teaching and Learning as Shared Inquiry

In classrooms where teachers join students in shared inquiry and where students' discourse is valued, teachers view learning as transformational. In those classrooms, teacher researchers hold common assumptions about learning and teaching. They agree on the following:

- Learning is social and transactional.

- Learning communities are complex systems.

- Spoken and written discourse mediates learning.

- Reflective inquiry fuels teaching and learning.

All of these assumptions suggest that we can find answers to our questions about teaching and learning in classroom talk and texts.

Learning Is Social and Transactional

Rosenblatt (1978) and Harste, Woodward, and Burke (1984) are just a few of the researchers who support the assumption that reading and learning are the result of transactions among people and texts within complex social and cultural environments. A transaction occurs when participants come together in a particular context for specific meaning-making purposes. New meanings result from the transaction, and in the process all the participants are somehow changed. A transactional approach to learning assumes that knowledge happens in the transactions among people and texts.

Each learner experiences complex transactions *within* himself or herself as he or she encounters questions or puzzles, reads and writes, and gathers new information to come to new understandings. As groups come together in shared tasks, the complexity multiplies. Learners enter into group transactions, and the energy level rises. Individuals may join with other individuals within the group and create two-person transactions *between* themselves. They may also join with several others in a single transaction to create learning transactions *among* the members of the larger group. All this interdependent and dynamic learning suggests that learning communities are dynamic, complex, exciting, and generative. One cycle of transactions sparks another and another. Networks of unpredictable meanings emerge from these learning communities.

Learning Communities Are Complex Systems

A second assumption common to teacher researchers is the view that learning communities are complex systems. Borrowing the concept of "complex system" from mathematics and the physical sciences, we see learning communities as multifaceted, dynamic systems that behave in nonlinear, interdependent ways. Many physical phenomena, like rocks and planets, seem to follow predictable Newtonian laws, exhibiting linear causal relationships among easily identifiable components or variables. Other phenomena, like the weather, ecology, and subatomic physics, are so complex that individual parts or variables are difficult to observe and measure. Predicting the behaviors of individual parts in these complex systems is almost impossible. These systems, like learning, are so complex that they have a constant element of unpredictability. We can see patterns across many classrooms or across time in one classroom, but trying to predict individual learning moments is futile.

Students' learning depends on how students see themselves, on their knowledge about the topic, and on how they plan to use this new learning. Learning depends on students' relationships with other students and with their teachers. It depends on students' life histories, their current feelings of security, and their sense of hope for the future. Teachers' decisions depend on student needs, curricular mandates, and the culture of their campuses. Teachers' knowledge is grounded in intuition, experience, research findings, and theoretical principles. Parents, community members, administrators, teachers, staff members, and students join these complex negotiations we call schooling.

This complexity means that there are no clear questions or simple answers, and small decisions can have significant and unpredicted effects. This complexity also means that change is a constant, context is critical, and important truths lie within the participants' perceptions. To study these learning systems, we must use approaches that recognize complexity and that can capture meanings from multiple perspectives across time. Classroom discourse embodies those complexities, and the records of that discourse are valuable for reflection and ongoing inquiry. By examining classroom discourse, we can study our learning, in spite of its confusing layers of complexity.

Discourse Mediates Learning

This leads to a third assumption common to the thinking of many teacher researchers: classroom discourse is critical to learning. When we view learning communities from a systems perspective, we see a complex network of transactions between and among individuals and groups, texts, and contexts. Discourse is the glue that holds this infinitely complex network together. Through written and oral language, individuals make, record, and present their unique meanings to others. In schools, we have generally used discourse for performance tasks designed to exhibit students' knowledge. Tests, recitations, reports, and essays are traditional forms of discourse for this type of learning product. In transactional classrooms, however, teachers and learners balance product and process. They use journals to discover what they know and conversations to present their ideas, articulate their questions, and share information. Sometimes the students use logs to record their inquiry decisions, to leave a paper trail for future reference and reflection. Often in these classrooms, students are encouraged to demonstrate their learning through an alternative sign system such as art, music, or drama. But even in those situations, oral and written language still serve to support and extend their meanings.

Like individual students, pairs and groups of learners also use language to articulate and record their emerging understandings for one another and for future reflection. Journals, logs, and diaries are invaluable records of individual learning. Taped conferences and conversations are important records of emerging understandings, discoveries, and questions. Without this talk and without these texts, our shared inquiry would be short lived. We would change, but we would not be able to study how and why. For example, working with my colleagues to explore the use of portfolios in teacher education courses was an exciting learning experience, but the written record of our initial transactions, the polylog, made it possible for us to revisit those experiences months later to enrich our understandings and provide springboards for new transactions.

Vygotsky's work (1962/1986) has shown that language links thought and action. Vygotsky suggests that learners participate in social action with assistance from more experienced learners, gradually becoming more independent and building the thought that moves the learning transactions forward. Language is central to this action-thought connection. Learners are immersed in language and use language for social interaction. Language plays a critical role as learners focus on new questions and unfamiliar contexts for continuing social action. When language and thought transact within particular contexts, learning happens and learners transform.

These kinds of learning transformations happen most routinely in environments rich with literacy and life experiences, opportunities for social action, and a climate supportive of risk-taking and problem-solving. These are sometimes called "abductive environments" (Harste, 1994) in which students are encouraged to make leaps from the known to the unknown, from the familiar to the new, from clarity into ambiguity. In these environments, discourse serves many purposes. Teacher researchers invite their students to help create classrooms filled with opportunities to ask questions, to look for answers, and to share what they know.

The teacher's role within these classrooms is becoming increasingly clear through research. Teachers work with students within their zones of proximal development (Vygotsky, 1962/1986). Teachers assist students with tasks that they cannot yet accomplish alone. Teachers ask questions and clarify issues that allow students to ask more complicated questions and explore unfamiliar concepts.

Reflective Inquiry Fuels Teaching and Learning

Finally, teacher researchers believe that inquiry drives learning in their classrooms. Learners' questions frame the tasks and structure the instructional time. Sometimes individual learners work on their personal questions and sometimes group inquiries focus student efforts. Teachers guide the inquiry, integrating required content as appropriate and responding to current student

knowledge by introducing more complex tasks.

In these classrooms, inquiry also drives teaching. Inquiry feeds the teachers' instructional planning, their responses to students, and their more general professional development. The discourse of inquiry is central to the life of these classrooms and is essential to students' growth, but it is also central to the learning of the teachers. These teachers also remind us that inquiry influences professional growth. Teachers join others to ask questions and search for answers, together finding no absolute answers but only better questions. Through this problem-framing process and their collective reflection, teachers "outgrow their former selves" (Harste, Woodward, & Burke, 1984) and move to new and often more significant professional action.

Teacher researchers also demonstrate that inquiry can drive curriculum development. A single teacher researcher negotiating curriculum changes within one classroom can use inquiry to make decisions. But at the campus or district level, curriculum development is more often by consensus. The result is often a document serving the requirements of the bureaucracy rather than the needs of the students.

Teacher researchers also teach us that time for reflection is a critical part of learning. Too often, the pace of classroom and campus activity does not allow teachers or students to pause and look at both the present and the future.

Teacher research requires this kind of time, and time is one of the major challenges for teacher researchers in both kindergarten through grade 12 schools and in universities. But we know that it is only through reflection that we can fully understand what we are currently doing, why we do it a certain way, whether it is what we want to do, and what we should do next. It is through reflection with our students and our colleagues that we come to collective understandings and build theory to guide our shared inquiries. This is true for groups of student learners as well. Through opportunities for group reflection, the learning community can move forward, informed by a knowledge of its history, values, strengths, needs, and goals.

Learning Through the Discourse

Classroom talk and texts may trace our initial learning, but reflecting on the records of the talk and texts moves us to another level of inquiry. My learning from the polylog was strengthened when my colleagues and I returned to the polylog's record of discourse to explore what it said about our learning. The power of what teachers have to say is strengthened as they review audiotapes, transcripts, and written records in order to explore additional meanings and as they join published researchers who have used records of classroom dis-

course to explore their teaching and learning.

For example, Paley (1989) has spent almost 20 years inviting her three and four-year-old learners to tell stories and act them out. She captures these stories on audiotape and then uses the tapes as the basis of her reflective writing. She listens to the tapes with a general question or focus in mind. She transcribes conversations that help her answer the question. Paley then writes stories of her learning, stories that inspire and enlighten wide audiences of teachers. Her close look at the rich discourse among these young children has generated important questions for her continuing teaching and learning journey and for ours.

Wells and his colleagues also watch students closely, focusing specifically on the oral discourse among teachers and learners during teaching moments. He and Chang-Wells (1992) focus on learning conversations in science classrooms and the literate thinking that supports students' learning of science concepts. Wells, et al. (1993) look at the rich potentials of collaborative research and reflection for school change and teacher professionalism.

Lambert's (1993) article "The Function of Anecdote in Teacher Research" reports about the power of conversation and storytelling among teachers who are trying to make sense of their classroom experiences. According to her, teachers' conversations play a critical role in our conceptualizing and reconceptualizing of experience. Through the telling of these anecdotes, teachers come to new and richer understandings of their experiences.

Hollingsworth's (1994) response to the complexities of helping beginning teachers was to organize regular social meetings where the participants asked questions and explored the issues involved in learning to teach. This teacher learning community met periodically for three years, using conversation both as their method of longitudinal research and as a means of support in learning to teach. Hollingsworth and her colleagues analyzed the transcripts of these conversations and then wrote narratives about the issues they had explored together.

Reliving the Learning

Classroom discourse makes clear our efforts to help learners link new information to old. Discourse within classrooms and in teacher workrooms captures learners' efforts to link thought and language to action and theory to practice. In both contexts, discourse captures the inquiry process and the products of the inquiry. Through discourse, we become communities of learners, and by studying our discourse, we can learn even more about the complexities of teaching and learning.

REFERENCES

Harste, J.H. (1994). Literacy as curricular conversations about knowledge, inquiry, and morality. In R.B. Ruddell, M.R. Ruddell, & H. Singer (Eds.), *Theoretical Models and Processes of Reading* (4th ed., pp. 1220–1242). Newark, DE: International Reading Association.

Harste, J., Woodward, V., & Burke, C. (1984). *Language stories and literacy lessons.* Portsmouth, NH: Heinemann.

Hollingsworth, S. (1994) *Teacher research and urban literacy education: Lessons and conversations in a feminist key.* New York: Teachers College Press.

Lambert, P.S. (1993). The function of anecdote in teacher research. *English Education, 25,* 173–187.

Paley, V. G. (1989). *White teacher.* Cambridge, MA: Harvard University Press.

Rosenblatt, L.M. (1978). *The reader, the text, the poem: The transactional theory of the literary work.* Carbondale, IL: Southern Illinois University Press.

Vygotsky, L.S. (1986). *Thought and language.* (A. Kozulin, Trans. & Ed.). Cambridge, MA: MIT Press. (Original work published 1962)

Wells, G., Bernard, L., Gianotti, M., Keating, C., Konjevic, C., Kowal, M., Maher, A., Mayer, C., Moscoe, T., Orzechowska, E., Smieja, A., & Swarts, L. (1994). *Changing schools from within: Creating communities of inquiry.* Toronto: Ontario Institute for Studies in Education Press.

Wells, G., & Chang-Wells, G. (1992). *Constructing knowledge together: Classrooms as centers of inquiry and literacy.* Portsmouth, NH: Heinemann.

CHAPTER 2

Allowing Space for Not Knowing: A Dialogue About Teachers' Journals

Marné B. Isakson and David D. Williams

Isakson has published several articles as a teacher researcher and has recently completed a doctoral dissertation focusing on literacy learning among reluctant and less proficient adolescent readers. She currently teaches reading and English at Timpview High School in Provo, Utah, USA. Williams is an associate professor of education at Brigham Young University, Provo, Utah. He encourages students to pursue inquiry projects as they teach in many different settings while exploring the use of teacher inquiry in his own practice.

Setting the Stage

■ One day in the fall of 1985 I was asking a colleague questions about my efforts to teach high school reluctant readers. She stopped me and said, "Marné, you are the one who has to make sense of what is going on in your classroom. Write what you see happening." Some suggestions she gave were: "Be specific and precise as you can. Look back at those observations and reflect on what you are learning. Think about what the events mean for instruction" (M. Siegel, personal communication, September 21, 1985). I took her advice and began my odyssey as kid-watcher. For five years I kept teacher journals on almost a daily basis by writing whenever I had a chance during class, between classes, or after school. I usually noted experiences with students who stood out in my mind, and I then explored my thoughts and feelings associated with those experiences.

During the last few years I have not kept the same kind of journal because the process seemed so time consuming. Instead I have experimented with alternative ways to record kid-watching by writing notes on seating charts and lesson plans, and keeping unwritten mental notes. I have not been as pleased with the results. Though I found ways to record observations, the chance to reflect in journal writing has had no counterpart.

I have begun to ponder the effects of journal writing on my teaching practice. As part of this pondering, I decided to take a thorough look at my journals to clarify why they were so valuable to me and why they seemed to be such a strong force in my evolution as a teacher. To help me clarify these experiences, I invited others to react to them. I wrote an interpretation (Isakson, 1992) of some of my journal-writing experiences using ethnographic analysis procedures recommended by Spradley (1980) and following standards outlined by Lincoln and Guba (1985). I shared parts of this document with several elementary and high school teachers who gave me written reactions. I showed my work, the teachers' responses, and my original journals to David Williams, a professor at Brigham Young University. I asked him to respond by asking probing questions and sharing some of his related experiences.

As a result of these analyses and sharing activities, we present a dialogue in which we explore various interpretations of our journal writing and analyses. We raise questions for ourselves and for readers to consider as we think together about the value of journal keeping by teachers.

A Dialogue

David

Briefly describe how you keep your journals and please give some examples.

Marné

The basic format of the 1985 journal was to write the date and what I saw happening. I kept a separate journal for each class in a spiral-bound 8 ½" x 11" notebook. I wrote in ink as I do any journal or daybook, because these writings represented who I was at that moment, so I wanted to save them. I see myself in a constant state of transition and find it interesting and helpful to reconsider past transitions. To give a flavor of that journal, here is a sample entry from Fall 1985 (all names except the authors' are pseudonyms throughout this chapter):

> Tom—came tardy—his 4th. During 15 min. of silent reading: Fiddled with his art supplies, pens, markers, putting them in bags. I whispered a question to him, "Do you know what you are to be doing now?" "Yes, I know." —2 more min. of fiddling. Then he started reading. He read 3 min. —looked around, looked at the clock, did not disturb others—but no reading. Got up 5 min. early to put book away. When I told him he couldn't but had to stay in his seat until the bell, he replied: "That's stupid. I'll leave it out then." He didn't put it away either. He didn't write in his journal for the 5 min. He had made a note earlier, three lines. Oh, the book he had selected

was C. Sandburg's Complete
Poems *[1970]. I would infer that
he wasn't interested.*

I kept all the journal entries together
in succeeding years and labeled the
entries according to class period. This
was more effective because the overall events for the day were often similar, and I did not have to repeat myself. The usual format was a
three-part entry: description of the
overall literacy events, observations
of specific students in those events,
and reflections on the significance of
the occurrences. This format helped
me learn about the students, conditions, and interactions so that I could
support the learners in my classroom.
The 1989 journal could best be char-
acterized as a notebook filled with
longer, more specific observations
and more pointed reflections than the
1985 journal. By then my reflections
had become interspersed throughout
the observations. If an idea occurred
to me while I was describing an observation, I did not wait until the
"Reflections" section because I might
forget the thought. So I put "OC"
(Observer Comment) and wrote my
thoughts immediately. Here is a sample entry from Fall 1989:

> *Literacy Events: Shared three young
> adult books—students were to list
> the ones they thought they might*

*like to read; read literature-study
books.*

*Observations: (OC) Quite by acci-
dent I stumbled onto something
that I plan to try again.*

*5th Hour: I didn't want to take the
time to write the titles and authors
on the board, but Cora wanted to
know them, so as I finished sharing a segment of a book, I passed
it to her in the front row. But then,
to my surprise she started passing
each book to the person behind her
who looked at it and passed it on.
I noticed that they read the jacket,
flipped through, started reading
parts. Jed pointed to the song of
one of his favorite rock groups. He
asked how he could get the book*
Rock 'n' Roll Nights *(Strasser,
1982). Winn and Erin spent quite a
bit of time looking in* Rock 'n' Roll
Nights *together.*

*(OC) Touching good books is a
good idea it seems.*

*Terri stayed after class to talk
about the child abuse in* Secrets
Not Meant to Be Kept *[Miklowitz,
1989]. Her friend had been sexual-
ly abused as a three year old by
her brother and his friends—gang
rape. She had blocked out the
memory until her brother came
back recently—the scars and
memories are coming to light as
they did for the main character in
the book.*

TABLE	CONTRASTING JOURNALS OF FALL SEMESTER 1985 WITH FALL SEMESTER 1989		
		1985	1989
equivalent number of pages		91	118
equivalent number of entries		53	56
number of pages with 3 or more entries (short entries)		24	2
number of pages with 1 or extended entries (long entries)		41	97

More recently, I have varied my journal-making in several different ways. For example, I created seating charts with boxes as large as I could make them for writing fieldnotes about individual students.

In the last few years, because of simultaneous doctoral work, I have neglected my notetaking. I write sporadically rather than daily, but the reduced practice is still rewarding in keeping me a learning teacher full of inquiry. Now that I finally have a computer in my room, I no longer write the entries out longhand in a spiral-bound journal. Instead I sit at the word-processor at the end of a day or during my planning period and write my observations and reflections. I do not do this consistently or on a chosen day; instead I write entries when I am in the mood to make observations. I find it helpful to tape a notecard to my desk to jot reminders of significant events I want to think about. This quick note usual-ly is made between classes or at odd moments during a class period.

David

It appears that over the course of five years, the length of your entries grew while the number of entries remained about the same (see Table). How do you account for that? And how do you find time to do all this writing?

Marné

I found time to write because I came to value the process. I considered it some of the best time spent preparing for teaching: I found time to write when the students wrote in their journals, between classes, during my planning period or lunch break, after school (the usual time), and in the evenings. If I did not write the observations immediately, I could not recall some of the more memorable stories. I did not let that bother me because there were many more stories from any class period on any day. I came to understand that the particular stories and events were not as important as the act of reflecting itself. Reflection helped me teach all my students more effectively, whether they were part of the event I reflected on or not. Because immediate recording was usually impossible, I tried memory-jogging strategies with varying degrees of success: *recording* notes on a 3" x 5" card in my pocket, on the seating chart, or in the margins of my journal; *pondering* the events of the day and writing what seemed salient; and *looking* at the list of names in the roll book at the end of the day to stimulate recall of events.

Following these principles, I wrote the stories in as much detail as time would allow. If I had only five minutes, that is what I would spend. If I was waiting for a ride, I would write. If something happened during the day that I felt compelled to explore, I would make the time needed; and sometimes that exploration for connections and insights took several pages. Sometimes I did not have time to reflect, but I did try to capture the event so I could think about it later.

David

How do you decide *what* to write?

Marné

I practice three general rules for deciding what to write.

1) I accept that I cannot see everything, so I select something that interests me.

2) I write what I actually perceive with the senses rather than interpretations. I concentrate on writ-

ing enough detail so the situation can be saved for future reflection and insight. Instead of "Marc seemed discouraged," I tried to write "Marc slammed his book shut, said, 'This is a stupid book,' and laid his head on the desk." After all, such an event could be interpreted in several ways. Place-holding the specific behaviors in this way allowed me to put additional information with this event so I could make sense of it and support Marc's literacy learning.

3) I try to see the situations from the point of view of the participants. This involves interviewing them, studying documents produced by them, talking to important others (parents, teachers, classmates) who have insights into their perspectives, and observing the whole situation. In the past, focusing too narrowly put blinders on me, so I missed the big picture of what was going on. I tried to consider the social climate at the time and anything else that could be happening to influence the student(s) I was observing. A useful question I came to ask myself was, "How might the student(s) I am observing see this event differently?"

David

Why do you insist on writing instead of just talking to others like many teachers do?

Marné

I *do* talk, but as valuable as it is, talking with other teachers does not suffice because it is too sporadic; it is based on the convenience of others (when I want to talk may be at a time that is an imposition on a colleague); we don't have time to get deeply into all the areas of concern I want to think about; colleagues are not always available when I have the time and inclination; and when teachers get together informally (at lunch or after school), they need a break from "talking shop."

Futhermore, writing for me is not just a substitute for talking to a colleague; it alone is extremely valuable. By analyzing the journals for the reasons I write, I discovered that writing invites moments of insight by creating a space in which I can make sense of my experiences. Writing also provokes thinking I otherwise would not do and prods me into uncomfortable areas that I would otherwise dismiss. As Macrorie (1987) suggests, "The journal's power to generate disturbance is to be celebrated rather than censored" (p. iii).

I also found that writing releases emotions and allows me to match words to what I am feeling. It forces me to deal with my emotions instead of letting them gnaw at my insides. Writing also "satisfies the defiant human desire to preserve certain 'unforgettable' perceptions against the an-nihilation of time" (Rainer, 1978, p. 56). This allows time for connections to develop that would not be made outside the act of writing.

In the following entry in my teacher journal from November 30, 1988, I wonder if the same could be said of learning to teach as well as learning to read:

> *Joe asked, "What good does it do to write about the book or to talk about it? Why can't we just read? This is a reading class isn't it?" I heard myself giving this answer: "It's by writing or discussing that meaning comes to your awareness. When you learn how to reflect on what you read, you have learned how to understand as you read. Of course, you won't always say or write these reflections, but as you do so in this class, this type of quality thinking will become natural for you, and you'll be a good reader." Joe seemed to accept this....*

David

What have you learned so far from your journal writing and analyses about keeping a journal as a teacher and being a teacher researcher?

Marné

The main lesson I have learned is that I use a journal to refine my thinking as a teacher. The analyses showed that through writing, I facilitate my own teaching in at least five ways, as cheerleader, peer-learner, detective, bookkeeper, and mentor/ friend (see the figure). My students need a facilitator to enhance their thinking and learning, and so do I. I am learning to use my journals to interview myself, to debrief my teaching, and to explore my own perceptions and conclusions more systematically. The figure illustrates ways I have been using the journals to inquire into my own performance as a teacher and into my students' world. This inquiry improves my efforts to facilitate both their learning and my own.

Journals Help Maintain the Self as Teacher

David

Tell me more about the *cheerleading* role and how it helps.

Marné

Many times before I began keeping a journal, I would come home from a long day of teaching feeling discouraged with myself. I lost sight of the good I was doing and spent all my memory energy on my mistakes, perceived weaknesses, and discipline problems. I found that keeping a journal served a cheerleading function by helping me record a wider array of events and not just my discouragements. On November 9, 1988, I wrote:

I feel really discouraged today— the feeling is force rather than choice. I need to turn this around. Today was a near waste during 4th period. Five boys wanted to lie on the floor to read. It hasn't worked in the past and so I wouldn't allow it. A fight all the time, esp. Cal and Bob.

Kent wants to keep giving up on The Book of Three *[Alexander, 1964], but Cal keeps talking him into it so they can be "reading partners" and Kent stayed with it but kept saying, "I don't get it. I can't figure out what is going on." Cal asked me on p. 31, "Who is Hen Wen?" During reading response groups I spent the whole time with them trying to explain the story so far.*

We went to the library to look for books we might enjoy reading. Kent just can't seem to get in gear. Everyone else seemed to explore. Jim said that he wanted to read Dune *[Herbert, 1984]— a huge book compared to the 60-page books he has been and is reading.*

José finished The Cay *[Taylor, 1976] and chose to read* Tom Sawyer *[Twain, 1883]. "I like reading books like this," he said, pointing to the* The Cay. *Peggy writes terrific responses to letters that others write to her.*

FIGURE   WAYS TO USE JOURNAL WRITING TO FACILITATE TEACHING

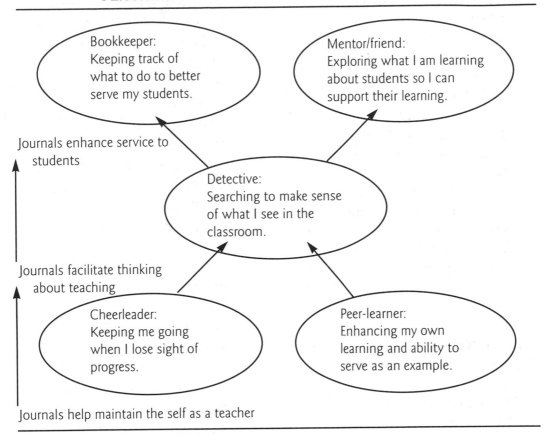

Bookkeeper: Keeping track of what to do to better serve my students.

Mentor/friend: Exploring what I am learning about students so I can support their learning.

Journals enhance service to students

Detective: Searching to make sense of what I see in the classroom.

Journals facilitate thinking about teaching

Cheerleader: Keeping me going when I lose sight of progress.

Peer-learner: Enhancing my own learning and ability to serve as an example.

Journals help maintain the self as a teacher

Before I started that entry all I could think of was how upset I was about the altercation with the five boys. As I started writing, I realized that learning and teaching had occurred in spite of this negative event. Cal had supported Kent to stay engaged with the book. Confusions and misconceptions were cleared up about a character. Jim had the courage to try a long book. I gained an insight about the effects of authentic writing for Peggy. José was obviously learning what he likes to read. On this day writing helped me see past my negative perspective to important events taking place.

I still needed to ponder the seating problem and decide how to handle this recurring situation next time, but

I was no longer demoralized by it. Cooper (1991) expresses this use of journals:

Journals allow us to examine our own experiences, to gain a fresh perspective, and by that means begin to transform the experiences themselves. I was startled by the power of this process. It is through telling our own stories that we learn who we are and what we need. (p. 99)

Celebration is also a part of the cheerleading role of the journals. In December 1993, I was reflecting on a wondrous breakthrough for a student. I noted why I wrote about that event:

I certainly had to capture it if for no other reason than to look back and say, "See, change in feelings toward reading can happen: Even the most reluctant can have highly charged and pleasurable reading moments." I need to remember this day, for it's easy to forget that my class and a good book can make a difference.

Self-talk helps a lot. Some of my journal entries are simply pep-talks, to gear myself up for what lies ahead or to keep myself going during difficult situations. Notice the coaching and cheerleading in the self-talk of this journal entry of August 1989:

I'm starting this year feeling nervous because more than ever I'm determined to move with the students, grab unscheduled opportunities, and follow their lead. I'm also committed to more "authentic" reading and writing. It's scary because each day is an unknown. It also holds the most exciting possibilities. Go for it, Marné.

It is interesting to me that I now gain sustenance from rereading my journals. I am not sure why. Perhaps the stories remind me what I have been through and that I can continue with renewed vigor and confidence.

Sometimes things happen that I want to share, but doing so might overwhelm a delicate relationship with a particular student (for example, Brad has climbed from reluctance to the edge of being excited about reading; my exuberance might push him back). An outside colleague probably wouldn't understand or be interested, so I explore these issues in my journal.

I also tell my own stories to impose structure to my often chaotic experiences (Grumet, 1988). I would like to share a poem from my journal in this regard. In it I vent my anger, frustration, and concern with a certain situation. I endured the situation, and writing this poem helped serve a cheerleading role. Through writing it, I discovered how to handle the situation for the remaining month of school.

Crowther

Crowther
tears me apart.

He shouts his profanities at me
while screaming inside
    at his car accident,
"This is a bull-shit class,"
"You're not fair,"
"You should do this and this
    not this and this."

He's on the brink
    of violence, wrath,
    a semiautomatic gunning the
    room
        and all of us.

He seethes.
He festers.

He's going to show us though
    (or himself).
He'll be vastly wealthy someday
    and then...
I'll regret
    reminding him ro read,
    asking him to tone down his
    blue language,
    walking away when I can no
    longer take his abuse.
I'll regret all that.

I must learn not
    to take him on.
It only enlivens his explosion
    and upsets me for HOURS,
    DAYS.

I must try
to let him be invisible,
to understand his white hot
bitterness
    and not shovel in fuel,
    and not give him one more
    thing to dislike about himself,

but give him a cool drink, even a
doughnut of goodwill.

Or just let him be
because he'd probably throw the
water in my face
and mash the doughnut to crumbs
    with a thousand pounds of his
    rage,
"Don't touch me!"
Crowther
tears me apart.
When will it end?
How can I help it end?

Another month of this seems an
eternity.

This poem, written when I was feeling crushed by frustration, helped me understand what I had to do. I asked him where he would most like to sit. He chose the corner of the room, off by himself. Of course, I tried not to let him see how pleased I was with that choice. Then I left him alone. I did not initiate any dialogue with him; I avoided eye contact; I let him be invisible, requiring nothing of him. If he made a derogatory remark, I did not hear it. He did remarkably well under these conditions. He turned in his weekly reading logs, brought his book and journal daily and used them faithfully, and was always on time. Furthermore, the next fall he made a special trip to my class to show me a letter he had received from Lee Iacocca in response to a letter Crowther had written telling Iacocca how much he had enjoyed reading his book and asking him some questions. I guess I learned that sometimes the best thing to do is go against my principles. In this case my overriding principle was my self-preservation, but fortunately, it was what he needed.

David

I can certainly relate to your experience. At the university level, I sometimes feel discouraged with my students or myself and have found that writing about my feelings often helps me get beyond the disappointment to think about possible solutions. For example, in a graduate class I invited the students to be creative in generating a final paper that would summarize what they had learned throughout the semester. One student responded by critiquing nearly every point I had tried to make throughout the course. My first reaction was to flunk her. But then I spent some reflective writing time exploring what she had actually done and why I was responding as I was. I ended up assigning her an "A" because I realized that she had understood what I was

teaching better than many of the other students and was able to persuasively call my views into question in ways I ought to consider seriously in subsequent offerings of this course. So, is this an indication that I was also becoming a peer-learner with my students?

Marné

By *peer-learner* I mean that I include in my journal some of my reactions to the things I am reading just as I ask my students to do. Through that process I interact more thoughtfully with the books I read and thereby respond better to my students' journal entries about their reading. Part of my role as a teacher trying to increase literate behavior is to demonstrate such behavior myself. When I have lived what I have taught, something interesting happens. What starts out for the purpose of demonstration for the benefit of my students, becomes me. I tremendously enjoy the thinking and interacting that are part of reacting to my own reading. Heath (1983) suggests that the most important condition for literacy learning is the presence of mentors who are joyfully literate people. And Calkins (1986) wrote, "Adolescents need teachers who demonstrate that reading and writing can bring tremendous joy to life" (p. 103). I knew that I had been successful in this regard when Kirsten said to me, "I know why we read in this class so much." I looked at her with great interest, and she continued "Because *you* love to read and want time to do it!" The following experience demonstrates this peer-learner role.

One year I had been reading *Last of the Breed* (L'Amour, 1987) while my students were reading silently. When it was time to write about their reading, I felt an overwhelming desire to write about what I had been reading, so I did. Up until that event, I had written with the students but I wrote about my observations and reflections on the class. This time I wrote as a reader. I wrote in the form of a letter to several students who were fans of L'Amour, and they wrote back. The experience was so enjoyable that I began writing regularly to students in a separate journal about my reading (Isakson, 1991). I was glad to discover this naturally from an authentic need as a reader.

Furthermore, I need to see what my students are going through. I need to be reading the same kinds of books and writing in the same genres as my students, and pondering the processes I go through in order to talk about reading and writing with insight and credibility. "The quality of teaching can only be enhanced when teachers think through the question of the nature of the learning process they want to promote in students" (Blue, as cited in Kaplan, 1987). The journals are tools for making my processing, as well as the joys and challenges of my reading and writing, visible.

David

This peer-learning role has been valuable in my teaching, too. In my graduate courses on qualitative inquiry I find that students not only benefit from seeing examples I am producing through my own ongoing inquiries, but they also provide valuable interpretive insights into analysis of my findings. In one case, a student could not believe that the high school program I was studying could be as wonderful as I was portraying it in my fieldnotes and in the draft conference presentation I shared with the class. So he decided to use his class project to interview others in the school and prove that my perceptions and conclusions were incomplete. I ended up encouraging him because I realized that many of the teachers and students in the school would tell him views they would not share with me because I was too closely associated with the program after studying it intensely for more than two years. His work completed my own study in many important ways.

Marné

Yes, and it is thrilling to see students learning from such interactions with teachers as learners rather than as "teachers." Perhaps we are teachers at our best when we are learners. In the following journal entry from November 1989, notice how Marshall has internalized my demonstration of collaborating for ideas from a few days before:

The most exciting part of the day was watching Marshall, Phil, and Jana's writing response group. Marshall confided in me before class, "I'm stuck. I just don't know where to go with it." I suggested that he do as I did with my piece of writing—ask the group for ideas. I, too, had been having the same block. Sharing my frustration with the class last Wednesday was the breakthrough for me. "Maybe your group can give you ideas." Later when I made it over to their group, Marshall had talked Phil into postponing his reading of his story so they could discuss Marshall's story. What transpired blew me away: Marshall read his story up to the "block" and then they just went crazy brainstorming what could happen. I said I'd cluster while they brainstormed. I looked at Marshall's paper and lo and behold, he'd already been clustering their ideas: I continued while the ideas were coming fast and furious. Then Marshall took over the clustering again. Before the class was over Marshall had some terrific angles he could take.

David

As I see it, these two roles of cheerleader and peer-learner help sustain you as a teacher by keeping you going emotionally and enhancing your own learning. Although the roles definitely benefit your students, they mostly seem to maintain you as a teacher so you can be more available to the students. Those seem like necessary but insufficient roles for a journal writing teacher. What about the second level of ways you use your own journals to facilitate your teaching , as shown in the figure: What is the detective role?

Journals Facilitate Thinking About Teaching

Marné

The third way I use journals allows me to think about learning and teaching. As *detective* I am constantly searching for understanding of my students by using clues they give me through their actions and responses to what I offer. The journal writing facilitates this search by helping me clarify what actually seems to be happening, the meanings students seem to be infusing into those events, and the meanings I am infusing. By writing, I am encouraged to think more systematically about these events and meanings. For example on October 5, 1993, I wrote:

We were having a writing workshop. Terri had written a poem about a dream, a nightmarish dream, but had left it in her locker. She asked to go get it. She brought back a decorated looseleaf binder in which she had beautifully preserved her poetry in plastic protectors. She has had many friends respond to the poem she wanted to show me and has reworked it herself. Her sister, "who is an English teacher," thought it was fine. So, [she wrote,] "I don't need to revise it. I like it just the way it is." She really is pleased with the piece. I asked if I could respond to it. She rejected each question or comment with "it is good how it is" when, in fact, she had used many general words and vague images.

I finally told her that perhaps she could write another piece that she wouldn't mind revising. [She said,] "I always like what I write the first time. My pieces don't need to be fixed up." They sound like she wanted them to sound; they said what she wanted them to say. Her writing could definitely be improved but she isn't a learner right now.

How could I support her as a writer: My fear is that she may have construed my comments as putdowns to her ideas and as a message that I do not like her writing. She is very private; she took the risk of letting me read this prized piece of hers. I desecrated it by calling parts of it into question.

How do I undo and move on to productive writing sessions for Terri?

I'll try to answer my own questions:

- Think how to respond to the individual so that she will feel encouraged to keep writing.

- Ask which lines or parts the student likes best. Ask where the parts are that she thinks are the weakest. Ask what she had thought of doing about those parts.

- Talk to her privately and tell her what I saw myself doing.

- Ask her how I can support her as a writer. Then do what she says.

- Include her in the discussion of other people's writing. Maybe she would do better revising others' writing. Keep setting up situations where, on her own and in her own good time, she can discover more interesting and vibrant ways to put language together. I could put up examples of vague, colorless sentences and have the class revise them.

- Be her cheerleader. She sees herself as a writer, and I must not do anything to diminish that view of herself.

- Ask her to respond to a couple of my poems that I consider unfinished.

- *Realize that Terri considers her piece finished, and I do not. Newman (1991) says if a piece is done from the student's perspective, consider it done. But Terri considers all her pieces "done" at first draft. I do not know how to help her.*

- *Structure the situation so she comes to a self-imposed desire to revise. What could I do—what kinds of authentic experiences might lead her to want to reconsider her pieces?*

In this entry notice the processes of my inquiry: I am puzzled; I wonder what to do; I describe what I see happening; I ask myself questions; I confront underlying assumptions about my duties as a writing teacher; and I brainstorm ideas for dealing with the situation.

Writing is a way to placehold my kid-watching for later reflection that may lead to insights about how to support learners or to revelations about underlying assumptions that deserve celebrating or that need changing or augmenting. I know from firsthand experience what Henke (1990) means about the pressures of teaching too often causing us to just get through the day, sometimes mindlessly, and about the power of the pen helping teachers reflect, conceptualize, and gain courage to experiment:

Teaching is such a busy profession that it is easy to fall into the habit of "just doing" without thinking about the doing. Active learners, however, need to reflect, conceptualize, and experiment. In order to learn about teaching, then, we needed to build in time and tools that facilitate the process. The professional journal seemed an ideal place to begin. (p. 283)

A journal can be a conversation with my evolving self. Snow (as cited in Weaver, 1990) wrote that we need to role-play ourselves into being the new kind of teacher we visualize; we need a period of self-regulated practice. A journal can help me work through my learning in these novice situations. Even though I have taught since 1968, situations occur daily in which I am a novice, doing things for the first time. Learning and making sense is always what I am about. I suppose I will always be in a period of self-regulated practice—perhaps that is what being in "professional practice" should mean.

Analyzing these journals has made it clear that I will always have something happening in the classroom that I will find unsettling and puzzling, including problems I think I have solved. I suppose those "sure things" change inevitably as my awareness deepens and expands.

David

I also find that keeping notes on my students and what I perceive they are doing and how I am helping or interfering gives me time and reason to think more carefully about them and my teaching. During a recent semester I was trying to teach an undergraduate general education class in a very different way—encouraging the students to take control of the curriculum as well as their own out-of-class applications of our discussions. It was a difficult experience encouraging them to take over the class while feeling I owed them direction. Writing about this experience for a journal article helped me think more insightfully and creatively about the experience than I could by just talking about it between class sessions to colleagues. This writing led to several changes in the ways I invited students to take responsibility for their own learning. Is this effort to apply my detective thinking and writing similar to what you are doing when you move to the third level in the figure?

Journals Enhance Service to Students

Marné

Yes, the third level represents an opportunity to put all the preceding thinking, discoveries, and insights into action to benefit the students and their learning. The term *book-keeper* refers to my use of the journal as a reminder of lessons I want to teach, guidance I need to give to particular students, calls I need to make to parents, and other tasks that constitute my teaching in terms of particular responsibilities I assign myself. For example, on November 9, 1988, I noted:

> *It is going to be hard to break Wes, Devin, and Darcy away from fantasy. Perhaps I'll try the "Books I Might Enjoy" stacks and lists tomorrow.*

On November 16, 1988, I wrote,

> *For "Harrison Bergeron" tomorrow, I'll ask them to retell what they know, list what puzzles them, list three questions they hope the author answers.*
>
> *Talk to Steve—why is he reading such easy things? Negotiate.*
>
> *Be an outside observer in one group per class tomorrow. They were not writing down all their good ideas. Why not? Discuss this with them.*

Basically, the bookkeeper use of the journal involves creating a to-do list, some items of which I act on and others I do not. For example, in Terri's story earlier, notice the "to-do" list. I started by putting up an overhead transparency of a poorly written, vague account of a scary event in which a jeep rolls backward toward the girl telling the experience. I asked the students to revise it with vivid images and action verbs. I gathered the stories, read them aloud, and asked for more suggestions to make this piece come alive for readers. Students participated very well, including Terri. The next day I brought two of my poems in rough draft form and asked Terri to respond to them.

Thus the bookkeeping notes of the October 5th entry were part of the brainstorming I did to try to solve the problem. I did not implement all the ideas immediately; instead, I asked two writing teachers for reactions to the story. Their input helped me decide where to begin. Continual kid-watching of Terri kept the decision-making process a dynamic one rather than one that was predetermined and concrete. The bookkeeper role of the journal keeps the possibilities for action before me so I am reminded and enabled to integrate them into my thinking and teaching.

David

I've kept notes on changes I wanted to make and students I needed to interview, but I never thought of those as being journal entries. I just thought that was formative evaluation that had to go on if I was going to tailor the class to the students taking it that semester. But I can see that by viewing these bookkeeping activi-

ties as part of a more comprehensive journal writing effort I might be more thoughtful about the whole thing by encouraging these plans for action to grow out of detective thinking. It could help me be more systematic in trying to understand the students as learners. How does the bookkeeper role merge into the mentor/friend role?

Marné

The *mentor/friend* role of journal keeping helps me focus on understanding my students as people. I wrote in my journal to learn from my students by trying to make sense of what I was seeing in my classroom. I had heard of Lucy Calkins, who had done an ethnography studying one child (Calkins, 1983). I had also heard of the Graves, Sowers, Calkins NIE project (Graves, 1983) in which they observed 16 children for two years in classrooms in the process of writing in order to discover how children develop as writers and how schools can help. These people were actually watching students and learning how to teach from them. Yetta Goodman's (1978, 1985) "kid watching" has had a big impact on me. The notion that I could learn how to teach by watching the students instead of only leaning on "experts" or finding programs was an empowering idea for me.

I discovered what Atwell (1987) meant when she wrote, "When I stopped focusing on me and my methods and started observing students and their learning, I saw a gap yawning between us—between what I did as language teacher and what they did as language learners" (p. 4). Writing down observations has helped me focus more on individuals. Insights would come, but conversely I would sometimes feel uncertain, confused, or overwhelmed about what to do to support a learner. I kept thinking about the situation, however. The only thing I could think to do at times was to interview the student to try to understand events from his or her perspective and then to collaborate in coming up with an answer. Perhaps this was the best thing to have done, because according to Harste, Woodward, and Burke (1984) "We have much to learn by using the child as our theoretical and curricular informant. 'The Child as Informant' is our call to the profession to go beyond kid watching to the active examination of current assumptions about language learning and instruction" (p. xvii).

Voss (1988) gained insight about the learning of her students by writing down her observations of their learning: "When most of the first graders in one class suddenly began collaborating with each other on original stories, I wrote about it in my journal and discovered some of their discoveries—and became more aware of the kind of help they needed from me" (p. 673). Likewise, my journals are filled with narratives about my students. Quite often these stories result in discoveries about how to support them, but always such entries help me see real human beings worth knowing and caring about—a valuable accomplishment given that I face more than 100 students a day. An example of an insight that led to learning is this entry about Kathy:

Kathy, who in the past has been unable to recall or retell what I read aloud, is capable of excellent listening comprehension. It has been so frustrating to me and to her that she can't tell back anything she's heard: Well, today I gave her a "listening helper" which I developed for her benefit. It has some questions for her to think about as she listens. I started worrying when she didn't write anything at all while I was reading aloud. But afterward while the rest of us discussed "Thank You, Ma'am," (Hughes, 1991) she wrote. She even added a piece of information to the discussion that no one else had offered—"She gave him $10.00, too." This participation in a discussion of a listened-to story is a first for her: The "listening helper" shows that she is capable *of understanding when someone reads to her.*

The event in this story was a breakthrough and worth recording, celebrating, and pondering for explanations in the context of my other writings about Kathy. This was the culmination of a long-term struggle we had been facing together to solve this problem. She wanted a solution as much as I. She had come to me on her own asking why she could not understand what I read aloud to the class. We made a discovery together, and the journal writing was critical to the process as well as the solution.

David

The notion of becoming a mentor/friend to students through writing a journal is fascinating. This role seems to be the ultimate reason for the previous four roles; fulfilling those roles culminates in meeting the mentor/friend purposes. In my own university teaching, maintaining myself through cheerleading and peer-learning puts me in a position to use my writing to play the detective role. What I learn as a detective is recorded in my bookkeeping notes for use with individuals and whole classes of students in supporting their learning as a mentor/friend. Thanks for helping me see how these roles fit together. The whole enterprise suggests that your research as a teacher has helped you become a better teacher. What have

you learned so far from your journal writing and analyses that has helped you understand teaching and yourself as a teacher?

Marné

I discovered that the act of struggling with these issues through writing has helped me realize that teaching is a transaction with unique people resulting in change of both student and teacher. The teaching/learning paradigm is a generative, caring act by both participants. Looking for a *set* answer for dealing with that delicate, unique learning moment is the antithesis of the *real* answer. The real answer is an uncomfortable one: do a "close reading" of the student and the social, psychological, and physical context. From information gathered through kid-watching, generate the supportive action to take.

The overall theme I discovered is that of teacher as learner. It might be stated this way: to teach well is to provide curricular support based on what I am learning about the processes of understanding my subject area and based on what I am learning about each particular student. Notice that I did not say "based on what I know about..." because knowing is sometimes construed as an absolute. In contrast, teaching is a dynamic process. In the place of the transposition modes of teaching ("I'll transport what I know into your head") are fundamentally different facilitative modes. In the facilitative teaching mode, both the teacher and student are asking authentic questions that perplex and excite; both are searching for understanding, making meaning, and trying to communicate what they are thinking.

This theme of teacher as learner has two features that seem to fit as underlying themes in nearly all the journal entries. The first feature is that a reflective teacher journal can help me learn how to teach better by making visible my assumptions, thereby helping me close the gap between lived theory and espoused theory. Second, a journal of observations and reflections of what goes on in the classroom and the meaning of those events can impact instructional decision-making and my ability to nurture the learners in my care (including myself as a learning teacher).

David

It seems then that the main thing you have learned from journal writing about yourself as a teacher is that you really can help individual students with their needs if you pay closer attention to them instead of thoughtlessly imposing your pedagogic methods on them. You have learned what it takes to be a mentor/friend and have realized that there is no single answer that fits every student in every situation, so you have to continually learn what the next student needs in a particular situation. You

have to be constantly open to really teach individuals well! What advice would you give to someone interested in starting this process with their own teacher journal?

Getting Started

Marné

"Just try," is what Judith Newman told me in 1988 when I was pressing her to find out everything first before trying a new strategy that sounded wonderful. I suggest teachers start slowly until they cannot stop themselves from writing about the amazing things going on in their classrooms. Currently, each sporadic opportunity to write an entry about an event on one day still leads to important insights for my teaching. Whatever amount of time can be given to observation, reflection, and writing will bring teachers to see what is right before their eyes. Newman (1991) calls the experiences one chooses for reflection on critical incidents, or "those occurrences that let us see with new eyes, some aspect of what we do. They might make us aware of the beliefs and assumptions that underlie our instructional practices" (p. 17). An inquiry stance is what it takes. I also recommend a few readings to generate enthusiasm and confidence for this venture: Goodman (1978, 1985), Fulwiler (1987), Newman (1988), and Isakson and Boody (1993).

How the Teacher Journal Pays Off

David

Is it worth all the effort to keep a teacher journal? Does writing in a journal make a difference in your teaching?

Marné

Is it worth it? My intuitive feeling is an overwhelming "yes." Some of the most dramatic and enduring changes in my teaching are a direct result of the observations and reflections in my journal. An especially poignant example is recounted in my work with Boody (1993). My student Bo and I seemed to be constantly embattled. We didn't see eye to eye on anything and were both convinced of our positions. My position was that he could enjoy reading and that some of the strategies I could teach him would make a difference. His position was that reading was worthless, that he didn't have time for it, and that he ought to sleep through class because he needed his rest for football. He was a classic reluctant reader, and I could not get him to engage in reading. I kept writing about him in my journal, trying to analyze my views and trying to see things from his perspective. I finally realized that I was part of the problem rather than the solution. He saw me as an authority

figure rather than someone trying to help him do something of value. I took myself out of the cycle and let other literacy invitations function in the classroom. A journal entry on November 30, 1989, shows the dramatic changes in Bo as a reader and in our relationship. The event took me by surprise, and I had to write about it. This was an unbelievable moment of celebration for me, one of the wonderful, cherished events that make all the months of struggle and frustration worthwhile:

> Bo was the most engaged in a book I've seen him all year. He asked me about five questions and would say, "Come look at this." Patrick, who is also reading Deathwatch (White, 1973), asked what page he was on. I was delighted to see the enthusiasm rubbing off on others—though not on Brady yet. Bo was trying so hard to picture the cliffs. He'd draw them with arm movements. He'd relate it to cliffs he'd seen. "How do you think it looks?" he asked. We read the description, trying to piece together the image. He stayed after class five minutes [he usually was the first one out the door] comparing Madec [a character in the book] to his own father as far as their abilities to hunt.

> This came up because suddenly Madec was shooting at Ben:

"How did Madec know where Ben was?" I asked.

"He's like my dad—a really good hunter." He then proceeded to tell me how his dad knows right where the deer will come and about what time. And he's right.

"How did he learn such things?"

"He's hunted all his life. He studies their movements, and he's talked to other good hunters. Plus he just observes things."

"Like Madec?"

"Ya! Madec figured out where Ben must have gone."

"Remember how Madec said he liked to hunt smart animals?"

"Ya! I wonder if he had this planned all along—to hunt Ben."

"Wow!" I said, *"We'll have to talk about that!"*

I have come to many insights about my teaching from reflecting on my experiences in the classroom. These have affected my teaching, so I believe writing in my journal has made a difference in my teaching. Some of these learnings are now an integral part of my daily approach to teaching. Other observations are much harder to put into practice consistently, which only further demonstrates the dynamic nature of teaching and my growth as a teacher. I am only partially convinced of the whole-

sale value of some of these teaching techniques and find myself using them as I believe they are appropriate for particular students in certain situations.

Telling the Story

David
Why tell this story?

Marné
First, I tell this story for me. Telling it helps me find out why I take the time to keep a teacher journal. I wanted to make visible the intuitive reasons for why I keep writing about the puzzling, intriguing, wonderful, or disheartening experiences of my teaching days. The transactional theory of reading (Goodman, 1994; Harste, Woodward, & Burke, 1984; Rosenblatt, 1978; Siegel, 1984) has strong parallels to what my journals do for me as a teacher. Just as readers transact with texts and both are changed in the process, I am changed by my transactions with the participants in the teaching situation and so are they. "The inferential processes we use to interpret the text or situation simultaneously change it and us" (Mayher, 1990, p. 283). Change is what reflective journals help us do. Boody (1992) says that teacher reflection has to do with change—"change of heart, change of being, change of actions" (p. 157). It also has to do with keeping what is good and knowing why.

The second reason I tell my story of keeping a teacher journal is that telling it allows me to share its values with other educators who might come to view the writing as time well spent and inquire into and reflect on their own practice. As Peshkin (1985) noted,

> My results invite other researchers to look where I did and see what I saw. My ideas are candidates for others to entertain, not necessarily as truth, let alone Truth, but as positions about the nature and meaning of a phenomenon that may fit their sensibility and shape their thinking about their own inquiries. (p. 280)

The third reason I tell this story about my experiences with teacher journals is political and spiritual and involves the first two reasons of self-knowledge and sharing with others. I believe teachers need to stop the "unquestioning compliance with curriculum guides, blind faith in instructional materials, impotence in the face of government and administrative edicts, guilt and anger about innovation, and lack of confidence as decision makers" (Nielsen, 1991, p. 1). Instead we need to build confidence in our own abilities to educate and to do what is right for the learners in our care. Since I have found journal keeping to be a powerful way

to get in touch with my professional self and learn from my experiences. I want to be a voice of support for my colleagues who are trying to risk a learner stance in their classrooms.

Marné and David

Using a teacher journal is a way to gain an inquiring, observant, reflective, and rejuvenating fascination for what goes on in our classrooms. Levine (1979) suggests the following approach:

> We're constantly building a new image of ourselves and wondering what's next. We have allowed ourselves very little space for not-knowing. Very seldom do we have the wisdom not-to-know, to lay the mind open to deeper understanding. When confusion occurs in the mind, we identify with it and say we are confused; we hold onto it. Confusion arises because we fight against our not-knowing, which experiences each moment afresh without preconceptions or expectations. We are so full of ways of seeing and ideas of how things should be, we leave no room for wisdom to arise. We desire to know in only a certain way, a way which will corroborate our image of a rational, separate, autonomous self. When we open our minds, our hearts, not trying to understand, but simply allowing understanding to occur, we find

more than was expected. When we let go of our ignorance and confusion, we allow our knowing mind to arise. (pp. 38–39)

Birch (1992) identifies a reality that many of us may have to face to become the kind of teachers we want to be:

Could there be something in the kind of thought that compels us to "pause to ask" that we are afraid may require more of us as people than we are willing to give? By pausing to ask are we not in danger of hearing something we may not want to hear? Something that may call on us to give—not just our time—but our souls: our care, our concern, our passion? And perhaps even more than this, our willingness to change in the face of those things we might see in ourselves—those realizations we might come to when we pause long enough, not just to still our bodies, but to also still our minds and hearts? Are we perhaps afraid of something within ourselves, something we are not sure we are ready to give up and so are not sure we want to face? If so, then the problem with reflection is not technical at all, but spiritual. (p. 2)

If we are willing to be teachers as learners, we all too soon will realize that "discovering who we are is to confront who we are not" (J. Preece,

personal communication, October 7, 1992). That is where learning begins. "Too often we find ourselves running away from something that we can't progress without. To sit still long enough, and listen close enough, and care enough to 'hear' the problem is already to be reaching into the solution" (Birch, 1992, p. 3). Journal writing may help you with this self-discovery as it has helped us.

REFERENCES

Atwell, N. (1987). *In the middle: Writing, reading, and learning with adolescents.* Portsmouth, NH: Heinemann.

Birch, J. (1992). *Reflecting on reflection.* Unpublished manuscript. Provo, UT: Brigham Young University.

Boody, R.M. (1992). *An examination of the philosophic grounding of teacher reflection and one teacher's experience.* Unpublished doctoral dissertation. Provo, UT: Brigham Young University.

Calkins, L.M. (1983). *Lessons from a child.* Portsmouth, NH: Heinemann.

Calkins, L.M. (1986). *The art of teaching writing.* Portsmouth, NH: Heinemann.

Cooper, J.E. (1991). Telling our own stories: The reading and writing of journals or diaries. In C. Witherell & N. Noddings (Eds.). *Stories lives tell: Narrative and dialogue in education* (pp. 96-112). New York: Teachers College Press.

Fulwiler, T. (Ed.). (1987). *The journal book.* Portsmouth, NH: Heinemann.

Goodman, K. (1994). Reading, writing, and written texts: A transactional sociopsycholinguistic view. In R.B. Ruddell, M.R. Ruddell, & H. Singer (Eds.), *Theoretical models and processes of reading* (4th ed., pp.

1093–1130). Newark, DE: International Reading Association.

Goodman, Y. (1978). Kid watching: An alternative to testing. *National Elementary School Principal, 57,* 41–45.

Goodman, Y. (1985). Kid watching: Observing children in the classroom. In A. Jaggar & M.T. Smith-Burke (Eds.), *Observing the language learner* (pp. 9–18). Urbana, IL: National Council of Teachers of English; Newark, DE: International Reading Association.

Graves, D.H. (1983). *Writing: Teachers and children at work.* Portsmouth, NH: Heinemann.

Grumet, M. (1988). *Bittermilk: Women and Teaching.* Amherst, MA: University of Massachusetts Press.

Harste, J.C., Woodward, V.A., & Burke, C. (1984). *Language stories and literacy lessons.* Portsmouth, NH: Heinemann.

Heath, S.B. (1983). *Ways with words: Language, life and work in communities and classrooms.* New York: Cambridge University Press.

Henke, L. (1990). quoted in C. Weaver. *Understanding whole language: From principles to practice.* Portsmouth, NH: Heinemann.

Isakson, M. (1991). Learning about reluctant readers through their letters. *Journal of Reading, 34,* 632–637.

Isakson, M. (1992). *A teacher keeping a journal: Touching the forces of teacher change.* Unpublished manuscript. Provo, UT: Department of Instructional Science, Brigham Young University.

Isakson, M.B., & Boody, R. (1993). Hard questions about teacher research. In L. Patterson, C.M. Santa, K.G. Short, & K. Smith (Eds.), *Teachers are researchers: Reflection and action* (pp. 26–34). Newark, DE: International Reading Association.

Kaplan, S. (1987). The teacher as learner. In G.L. Bissex and R.H. Bullock (Eds.), *Seeing for ourselves: Case-study research by teachers of writing* (pp. 41–58). Portsmouth, NH: Heinemann.

Levine, S. (1979). *A gradual awakening.* Anchor Press.

Lincoln, Y.S., & Guba, E.G. (1985). *Naturalistic inquiry.* Newbury Park, CA: Sage.

Macrorie, K. (1987). *Twenty Teachers.* New York: Oxford University Press.

Mayher, J.S. (1990). *Uncommon sense: Theoretical practice in language education.* Portsmouth, NH: Heinemann.

Newman, J. (1988). Journals: Mirrors for seeing ourselves as learners, writers and teachers. *English Education, 20,* 134–156.

Newman, J. (1991). *Interwoven connections.* Portsmouth, NH: Heinemann.

Nielsen, A. (1991). *Reading and writing our professional lives: Critical reflection on practice.* Course announcement. Halifax, Nova Scotia: Mount Saint Vincent University.

Peshkin, A. (1985). Virtuous subjectivity: In the participant-observer's eyes. In D. Berg & K. Smith (Eds.), *Exploring clinical methods for social research* (pp. 267–281). Newbury Park, CA: Sage.

Rainer, T. (1978). *The new diary: How to use a journal for self-guidance and expanded creativity.* Los Angeles, CA: J.P. Tarcher.

Rosenblatt, L. (1978). *The reader, the text, the poem.* Carbondale, IL: Southern Illinois University.

Siegel, M.G. (1984). *Reading as signification.* Unpublished dissertation. Bloomington, IN: Indiana University.

Spradley, J.P. (1980). *Participant observation.* New York: Holt, Rinehart and Winston.

Voss, M.M. (1988). The light at the end of the journal: A teacher learns about learning. *Language Arts, 65,* 669–674.

Weaver, C. (1990). *Understanding whole language: From principles to practice.* Portsmouth, NH: Heinemann.

Literature Cited

Alexander, L. (1964). *The book of three*. New York: Henry Holt.

Burroughs, E.R. (1923). *Tarzan of the apes*. New York: New American Library.

Herbert, F. (1984). *Dune*. New York: Putnam.

Hughes, L. (1991) *Thank you, ma'am*. Mankato, MN: Creative Education

L'Amour, L. (1987). *Last of the breed*. New York: Bantam.

Marshall, C. (1987). *Christy*. New York: McGraw Hill.

Miklowitz, G.D. (1989). *Secrets not meant to be kept*. New York: Dell.

Sandburg, C. (1970). *The complete poems of Carl Sandburg*. San Diego, CA: Harcourt Brace Jovanovich.

Strasser, T. (1982). *Rock 'n' roll nights: a novel*. New York: Delacorte.

Taylor, T. (1976). *The cay*. New York: Avon.

Twain, M. (1983). *Tom Sawyer*. Austin, TX: Raintree Steek.

White, R. (1973). *Deathwatch*. New York: Dell.

CHAPTER 3

Building a Reflecting Classroom

Franca Fedele

Fedele has been teaching for nine years and is presently working with the Peel Board of Education in Toronto, Ontario, Canada. She has been doing action research in her classroom for more than four years, offering her class a range of opportunities for reflection as she and her students share the value of the process. She recently completed the Masters of Education at Ontario Institute for Studies in Education in Toronto.

I learned that I work better with a partner than in a small group. In a small group if one person is not cooperating then the rest don't cooperate and that is frustrating. What I enjoyed most about this project was working on the play we did to show about Inca life. I like acting a lot. I need to improve my work habits by contributing more of my ideas. This is hard for me to do in a big group. (Meagan, grade 6)

■ In this written report we can see that Meagan has learned a great deal about herself. She has focused on her learning and is now able to identify some of her strengths and areas to which she needs to pay attention. This reflection did not come spontaneously. It was written af-

ter our class had spent several months reflecting on a variety of topics, using a variety of methods.

With my increasing involvement in action research, I find that reflection plays an increasing role in my professional life. As I reflect, I see the value of the process, and I share the act of reflecting with the students in my class. As the students become involved with reflection I realize it is worthwhile to them, so we reflect more often both together and separately.

Teacher Reflection

I have always spent time reflecting on my teaching. Most of this reflection is a mental playback of the day, the kind that many teachers experience. It is useful as a way of deciding how to proceed based on past events, thinking of solutions to problems, sparking new ideas, and dwelling on an unpleasant event in the hope of feeling better about it.

Another form of reflection occurs as I document the events of the day, observing student behavior during various activities and recording anecdotal notes. However, as I record, I think about what this observation reveals to me about each child and the activity in which we participate. This type of reflection helps me assess the student and my program. Schon (1988) refers to this behavior as "reflection on action." It helps me with planning and pushes me to examine my role in the classroom and how well suited my teaching strategies are to the individual students in my class. Based on this reflection I then record further program plans.

In recent years my reflection has been deeper. I continue to consider what I have done, how my teaching has affected the students, and what I would do next time. I am also looking at why I do what I do. I am considering my beliefs about learning and teaching, while trying to reveal my "hidden assumptions," as Newman (1987) would encourage.

As I have become more centered on my beliefs about teaching and learning I can better focus my thoughts. I now spend time considering specific details of my teaching, which makes my reflection more constructive. This kind of reflection

has been encouraged through reading material about my profession and through discussions with my peers. My personal interest in professional development has involved me in teacher inquiry. The audiotapes, videotapes, and transcripts collected during my inquiries have provided me with a wealth of information. Having concrete examples to examine independently and with colleagues has objectified my teaching and allowed me to be more critical and provide supporting evidence for my theories.

Through these experiences it became clear that reflection is a critical aspect of learning and consequently necessary for better teaching. I began to think that if students were given the opportunity to reflect, their ability to learn and their understanding of learning would improve. New understandings could then guide future learning. "We undertake reflection, not so much to revisit the past or to become aware of the metacognitive process one is experiencing but to guide future action" (Killion & Todnem, 1991, p. 15).

Student Reflection

My understanding of reflection as a learning tool developed over time, and, as it was developing, I was already unconsciously encouraging student reflection. Now student reflection is a conscious part of my program and takes place in a variety of forms across the curriculum.

Audiotapes and Videotapes

I began audio- and videotaping students while they were at work. When I analyzed these tapes I was often surprised, intrigued, and sometimes puzzled by what I saw and heard. I found that any amount of my independent reflection or discussion with a colleague would result in more questions than answers.

Although the questions raised by the tapes were worth pondering, it soon became apparent that more evidence was necessary to develop understanding. The best way to gain the necessary information seemed to be by showing the videotapes and audiotapes to the students. The students could then be asked why they went about their day as recorded on the video.

The students were provided with the time to listen to audiotapes or view videotapes. They were also given a transcript of the tapes. While they watched and listened to the tapes they were asked to fill in any information they thought was missing. Students then were given the opportunity to discuss their observations. This follow-up discussion was also audiotaped for further reflection.

This process was fascinating, because students could provide pertinent information. For example, they could tell me why they went about a task a certain way or what they meant by what they had said. More important, by watching and hearing themselves on tape, the students became aware of how they functioned in the classroom. The following is a partial transcript of a student's audiotape discussion with the teacher. The conversation took place after a group that had worked on a project together had viewed their tape.

Marty

We could have got a little more work done.

Teacher

What makes you think that?

Marty

We were arguing about stuff that has nothing to do with our work. We were fooling around.

Teacher

What else can you tell me from this part of the tape?

Marty

We weren't cooperating.

Teacher

Can you tell me when you weren't cooperating?

Marty

We were always correcting each other on everything. And mocking each other.

Through watching videotapes of their work sessions and discussing their impressions with me, students could examine their relationships with peers, their interactions with the learning materials, their work habits, their problem-solving skills, and their ability to express ideas.

Students were given the opportunity to observe a portion of their social, emotional, and cognitive development. This experience easily led to discussion of the various aspects of behavior that they noticed. With their peers, students could identify specific ideas and behavior that they liked or disliked. Their comments often went further, explaining why they disliked certain actions. Students would spontaneously discuss what they could do the next time they were faced with a similar situation. For example, the following comments were meant to improve the staging of a skit students were videotaping for a school assembly:

Darren

Katherine, you should sit down in a chair or something. Like right beside the thing (referring to the microphone).

Katherine

You couldn't see us. When you were on (referring to Clinton) and I was on, you couldn't see us. We were off to the side.

I realized that by viewing or listening to the tapes, the students were making all the observations I had made. Further, the tapes objectified their participation in the learning process, allowing them to analyze their learning as they allowed me to analyze my teaching. The tapes helped me make decisions about my teaching and allowed my students to make decisions about their participation in the learning process.

This reflection on students' actions during group work was valuable. I employed it to assist students to develop their awareness of how they interacted with their peers, how they went about completing a task, and how they presented their work. The students seemed satisfied with this kind of reflection. They were always pleased to watch themselves on videotape and were impressed when they were handed a transcript of their discussion. They discussed their observations in great detail. Often students would view the tapes, critique their work, and ask for the opportunity to redo the piece of work. By reflecting on their past work and how they could improve it, they made a better product the next time. This process was far more motivating than any lesson I could have taught or evaluation I would have given.

Think Books

Through my research I encountered a chapter titled "Making Sense in Journals, Learning Logs, Think Books" (D'Arcy, 1989). This work documented student use of journals to record their thoughts and encourage them to become more aware of their thinking processes. Through the reading of this chapter and the discussion that followed, I became acutely aware of the power of writing to increase one's learning. Through their own writing and the responses from their teachers, the students learned not only about subject matter, but also about themselves.

This reflective work seemed valuable. It made sense to me that keeping a journal, or notebook, with a collection of personal thoughts would be a useful tool for reflection. I implemented this form of journal keeping in my classroom. I accepted students' writing in the journal in draft form. Students were expected to record the thoughts they had as the events of the day took place, rather than simply listing the events.

The "Think Book" (the name I chose for the blank notebook I use for the journal) was introduced to the students as a place to record personal thoughts. They were encouraged to record ideas in written or pictorial form. It could be used at any time during the day and could be referred to for ideas for writing, discussions, and research projects. In addition, 10 minutes was set aside almost every day specifically for working in the Think Book. During this time everyone in the classroom, including me, would sit in silence and record their thoughts.

During Think Book time I sometimes asked the students to reflect on a certain topic. This input from me was meant to help children break away from using the book in only one format (such as a diary or list of events). Occasionally I specified whether the students should portray their thinking in writing or pic-

tures. This structure was imposed to encourage all students to work in a variety of forms—the reluctant writer to write occasionally and the reluctant sketcher to express thoughts pictorially. I hoped that exposure to these different styles would broaden the students' repertoire of skills.

The Think Books encouraged the children to consider what they were thinking. When the books were first introduced, entries tended to be brief and generally began with the phrase: "I am thinking about." The following entry was the first entry in Allison's Think Book: "I was thinking about recess and what we do at recess is play baseball." As the year progressed and the children became comfortable with this mode of reflection their entries became more focused and detailed. Students were not only recording their thoughts but also reflecting on those thoughts. The following is an entry Allison, grade six, made in April after reading a novel in which one of the main characters dies.

I remember when my cat Mick died. It was two years ago. On Easter morning my mom and I got up early. My big brother was watching T.V. in his room and my dad was working. Mick was crying because he wanted out, so my mom told me to let him out, so I did! About ten minutes later my mom let him in. All of a sudden we heard a thud. My mom pulled

*back the couch and there was
Mick, lying on his side, panting
and crying. I started to cry. My
brother phoned the neighbors. I sat
there beside Mick crying so hard,
telling him not to go. The neighbors and my mom quickly drove
him to the vet. My brother stayed
home with me. I believed Mick
would be alright, but when my
mom walked in the door without
Mick and she had tears in her eyes
I knew he was gone and never
coming back.*

*That was it, my favorite cat that
kept me company, protected me,
gave me hugs and snuggled with
me at night, was gone. I burst out
in tears. I couldn't believe he was
gone. For two years I was grumpy
on Easter. I thought it was my fault
he died. I also thought if I hadn't
let him out this wouldn't have happened. But now I know it's not my
fault. I miss him, but I'm not
grumpy on Easter!*

This entry demonstrates Allison's ability
to relate an incident from a novel to her
own experiences. In retelling her experiences she reflects on her feelings of loss,
sadness, grumpiness and guilt. She also
expresses how those feelings changed
over time and her new perspective on
the death of her cat. This reflection on
her personal experience of death helped
her relate to some feelings expressed by
other characters in the book.

After each Think Book period students were given the opportunity to
share what they had written. When we
began these sharing sessions I reminded
students that in our classroom no one
was to comment or snicker at anything
shared. I did this to enable them to
share thoughts safely without judgment
from others. In addition, I hoped to develop my students' abilities to listen
without feeling the need to impose personal ideas or judgments on others.

As the year progressed and most of
the students felt confident sharing their
journals with the class, we opened the
sharing sessions for discussion. The discussions that occurred varied in length:
on some days there were no comments
about student or teacher sharing, but on
other days several sharing topics were
discussed. The discussions were usually
focused and students gained insights by
bouncing their ideas off one another.

As I read the student Think Books, I
discovered a great deal of reflective
thought. Many students returned frequently to the same issues. The following excerpts show that Laurie, grade
four, seemed to be focusing on problems she was dealing with in her life:

5/6/93

*Last night we had a performance
and it was great, but I had stage
fright and couldn't even budge.*

5/6/93

One big problem that I have is not being able to see my dad or sisters. I really miss them a lot, especially my sisters. They're so young and they always depended on me.

5/7/9:

One big problem I had is when I got into fights, with Charlie and Casey. But I always had a way to solve the problems and be friends again.

5/12/93

Yesterday I had a big problem and that big problem was Tim because he would always start a fight.

Part way through the year I began to correspond with the students in their Think Books. I began to do this to encourage sustained thought on one topic. Most students responded to my entries. The focus of my correspondence was taken from the child's entry. The following is an excerpt of an ongoing reflection between Milton, grade five: and me on a book used for read aloud, *Garth and the Mermaid* (Smucker, 1992):

Student Entry: I think the book is good. Some parts are boring and some parts are exciting. There was one part I found exciting was when Garth wouldn't open his eyes and wake up.

Teacher Entry: What do you think makes a book exciting?

Student Entry: What makes a book exciting? My answer: if it has Fantasy, Adventure, Paranormal activity, just something that normally doesn't happen. What this book is missing? My answer paranormal activity and fantasy.

Teacher Entry: Isn't Garth going from Guelph, Ontario to medieval England, fantasy? I think it is. It is not science fiction, but anything happening in the imagination could be considered fantasy.

Student Entry: From the discussion (class drama based on the novel) that we just had, I think you're correct. It is a fantasy story. If I was Garth my wish would be to steal from the rich and give to the poor. Today our discussion was very intriguing.

These entries show that my responses were based on whatever Milton had written. In this case I posed several questions to encourage him to reflect on his comments about the novel. Milton responded in a way that demonstrates that he had reflected both on the events of the novel and the questions posed. When he changed the subject of his correspondence, I did the same.

Still later in the year I encouraged students to share their Think Book entries with a partner. They each responded to their partner's entries. Many students found this to be a difficult task. Responses were often brief and a topic was rarely sustained over more than a few entries. I hoped that this would change as students had more experiences reflecting in a written format. My observations suggested several reasons for the difficulties they had corresponding to one another. First, the activity was still new to them, and time was required to feel comfortable with it. Second, my students had a wide range of reading and writing abilities, and they may simply have had difficulty reading each other's entries or felt self-conscious about writing to their partner. Third, as a teacher, I too am challenged by trying to create an authentic response for some students' entries. My students may, therefore, also have been finding it difficult to think of something to say to their partner that relates to what their partner had written.

This aspect of the Think Book portion of my program requires further study. I need to speak to the students about their thoughts and feelings, speak to other teachers about their findings, and then do more professional reading about dialogue journals. I will also need to observe my next group of students and see how they respond to this portion of the program.

Written Self-Evaluations

Written self-evaluations were a part of our classroom throughout this school year. The research on reflection makes it clear that "To learn for understanding, students need criteria, feedback, and opportunities for reflection from the beginning of and throughout any sequence of instruction" (Perkins & Blythe, 1994, p. 7).

As previously discussed, students recorded regularly in their Think Books. Much of what they wrote was a reflection of their thoughts or actions, but I also felt the need to have students specifically focus on certain assignments. To achieve this, at the end of each large unit students were given the time and direction to independently write about their work. I asked them to respond to the following questions:

- What did you like about this assignment?

- What did you dislike about this assignment?

- What did you learn about yourself while working on this assignment?

- Which skills did you develop while working on this assignment?

- What did you do well on this assignment?

- What would you change next time?

This format for self-evaluation was used for novel studies and research projects. As the year progressed student self-evaluations became more rigorous. In November, after completing a visual novel study (a novel that is presented on videotape in an abridged format) and the corresponding activities, James, grade six, wrote:

> I thought the movie was boring. It was hard to understand the accents. My work was okay, but it could be better.

In March, after completing a novel study for a self-selected book, the same student wrote:

> I think I could have worked harder or tried harder at the beginning of the novel study. My effort improved as the deadline got closer. I think I wasn't motivated until I saw people ahead of me. Again my habits and enthusiasm also improved and got more fun as it went along. I only used my reading record sheet when I was reading, but I did use my checklist and I had 4 pages of jot notes. I thought that the best part of my novel study was how I used my resources because I used the dictionary and my PARENTS. My neatness is still average along with my punctuation however, my spelling I thought was great. I think even though my neatness wasn't great it's getting better especially my handwriting. I wasn't organized at all but I never was. I would improve my grammar and probably my effort. I like how everything made sense and how I really worked hard when the deadline got close. I learned that I tend

> to dodge the effort a bit but when I see a challenge I never turn one down! I also learned you have to really be up to it to get anything done.

This entry shows that James had developed the ability to focus more on the questions posed for self-evaluation. He had also begun to add details that allowed me to understand what he has learned about himself and the process he went through to complete the activity. The ideas I presented for the students to consider during self-evaluation had not changed. What had changed was the student's increased ability to reflect on his work. As confidence and skill developed, ideas became more specific and detailed.

Whole Class Oral Reflection

Over the past five months, in addition to audiotapes, videotapes, transcripts, Think Books, and self-evaluation, my students have engaged in the process of group oral reflection. This group activity was added to the program because it offered another opportunity for contemplative work.

The idea of reflection through talk was developed through whole class discussions. I felt this was a step toward developing children's abilities to participate in group discussion independently, without the teacher's guidance. This process also allowed me to once again reinforce the parameters for group discussion. I explained that the class should accept others' ideas and discuss the ideas constructively, but that sarcasm, ridicule and put-downs are not acceptable. Through research about teacher reflection I knew that teachers needed to feel safe in their environment to honestly discuss their work, feelings, and questions; such an environment promotes growth. Safety in this case "refers to an environment in which teachers can think about their work and concerns without fear of evaluation or judgment" (Richert, 1990, p. 512). I believe that students also deserve a safe environment for reflection; otherwise, true reflection cannot and will not occur.

After a work session, when the whole class had been involved in the same activity, we would gather for approximately 10 minutes. My goal was to have students share their experiences with other students. I felt that this would give them the opportunity to learn about their peers' ideas and techniques. Through discussion, I hoped that the students who were sharing their ideas might also gain greater insight about their own thinking.

We began group reflection by gathering after writing sessions, which we had spent focusing on poetry. I asked the students not to share their poems, but instead their thoughts about poems and poetry writing. The first sessions were extremely quiet. Research has shown that teachers require time "for reflection (including) having the time to establish rapport with a partner" (Richert, 1990,

p. 511). I feel that students also need this time to establish rapport.

I was providing the time for reflection, and I was assuming that the rapport had already been built; however, people do not always transfer skills, attitudes, and concepts from one area of their lives to another. I did not try to break the silence during our first few sessions. I felt that if I waited, the students would be forced to respond. I also wanted to avoid the possibility that I would dominate the conversation. One or two children would offer ideas shyly when they realized that I intended to wait until someone spoke. By the third session I knew I had to take action to make the students more comfortable. I did not want them to sit through the sessions without sharing. I needed to ease the tension surrounding this unknown aspect of the day. If this time became associated with discomfort it would not be conducive to reflection.

The next poetry discussion opened with two specific questions, which we used repeatedly for the next few sessions to provide a consistent structure. I hoped the familiarity of the questions would help the students formulate ideas to share. The questions were: "What did you learn about poetry?" and "What did you learn about yourself while writing poetry?" More students could participate in the discussion now that they had a sense of the direction it would take. Through these reflection times, students discussed a variety of poetry formats, rhyme, syllables, and topics for poems and the history of poetry formats. They also discussed how poetry made them feel and react.

I concluded that these two questions were good questions to open a discussion. They provided students with a focus and yet were general enough to be applied to each individual's experiences. Both questions considered the students and the skills the students were exploring, rather than the content of the poetry. This focus provided the reflective tone to the discussion. These questions were adapted for use during other reflection times as well. When the students were involved in research, the questions were "What did you learn about doing research?" and "What did you learn about yourself while doing research?"

Now with a familiar format, more students became involved in discussions. It was exciting to hear them share research strategies, discuss the way they solved problems, and pinpoint specifics about their learning styles and their feelings while participating in this kind of learning. It was even more exciting when I saw evidence of other children enhancing their learning by trying out an idea heard in a group session. For example, one of the students, Eric, was doing a project about Japanese involvement in World War II. While working on CD-ROM he found that there were many pages with information about World War II. Because he did not feel he could possibly read these pages, the librarian

showed him how to narrow his search by using Japan as a cross-reference. He was delighted that he had learned a new skill that would make his research easier. The next day another student solicited Eric's assistance in order to narrow her search on the CD-ROM.

So many good ideas and topics came up during these 10-minute reflection periods that we sometimes were unable to work with an idea in depth. Often I felt a student's thoughts were not given the time needed for discussion because other students were so eager to share their idea that they did not follow up on someone else's thoughts. I decided at this point to have written reflection precede discussions. I asked the children to write about their experiences with research and share these reflections with me. This technique would also give me a glimpse of the thoughts of the students who were not speaking during our group sessions.

The written reflection at this time proved to be a critical growth point for us. It provided a focus for further reflection, and it set us to the task of cooperative problem-solving. At this time I learned that I need to insert a regular class period, perhaps weekly, for written reflection when engaged in a large project. I also relearned that it is important and valuable to return the problem to the students and seek collective solutions. The students learned that it is acceptable and appropriate to let the teacher know when they felt a group member was not participating well. Students also practiced sharing specific feelings with group members, and they learned how to behave more assertively with unproductive group members.

The issues raised in students' written reflections became the areas of discussion for our next session. Instead of using our usual questions, I introduced the major issues raised in the written reflections, without identifying specific students. The discussion that followed involved many students. They did not discuss experiences because they did not want to reveal what they had written; the students therefore moved beyond this level of discussion and tapped into their beliefs about learning. The discussion centered around expectations of group research. Then the discussion turned to possible strategies for aligning what was happening with what they thought should be happening. We also discussed the setup of this research project. We listed the advantages and disadvantages of following school board–prepared questions and the feelings students have about deadlines. This session lasted 30 minutes; then the students broke up into their research groups to address issues and try their own strategies. Five months later, the students still look forward to our group reflection and express disappointment if we do not have time for it.

I have added two more questions to our repertoire: "Have you found any patterns while researching?" and "Did anything puzzle or surprise you?" These two questions are borrowed from Chambers' (1985) ideas for getting students to respond to what they have read. These questions help students reflect on both the content and the process of their work. At this point, however, the students could probably hold a reflective discussion without the support of the questions. They are now sharing enthusiastically, with a greater number of students participating in each discussion.

Small Group Reflection

I was feeling successful with the large group reflections, the clarity of my own thinking, and the students' thinking. However, I did not apply what I had learned from the large group discussions to what was happening during small group work time. In this case, I learned that children, like adults, require time to reflect, a focus, a feeling of safety, and the expectation to reflect.

I was sending students to work in small groups because I believed they interacted with one another more often in small groups; therefore, I was assuming more reflection would occur in these groups. However, I was not providing the structure for reflection to occur. I was assuming that by modeling it in a large group and suggesting they consider reflection in small groups, the students would reflect. Now I have data that show reflection did not occur.

As a result I have become more prescriptive for some of the small group work reflection period. Students reflect in writing; issues and strategies are discussed as a whole class; and then students are given the opportunity to reflect in their smaller work groups about the large group discussion. This procedure has worked very well.

I recognize now that modeling for the groups had not been enough. They still needed support which was provided through the two ingredients of specific reflection time and a focus for their discussion. I also built this activity into the timetable. For the next major project students were given the opportunity to reflect in both whole class and small groupings.

What Do Students Say?

The students and I discussed the value of reflecting on learning. Although they looked forward to our group reflection, they almost unanimously said they did not find any value in it. They did not mind the discussions and even liked them when we discussed specific issues. They felt small group reflection helped them solve some problems. They also did not mind doing written self-evaluation, but saw no value in it. Students did like their Think Books and rarely had difficulty deciding what to write. They definitely did not want to end their work in the books.

This information raises further questions. If the students do not value the reflection, is there something I can do to demonstrate its value? Are they simply enjoying the oral reflection time because it is not their "work"? Should I be allotting more specific class time to Think Books because I can see their value and students clearly like having them and interacting with their thoughts in this format?

Final Reflections

Being involved in reflection is an important part of learning. "Taking time and energy to reflect on and improve one's work are essential to the understanding process itself" (Simmons, 1994, p. 23).

The students in my class have been introduced to several methods of conscious reflection. During the year reflection was introduced more formally and more often in a variety of ways. I am certain it has had a positive effect. The students' reflections and work are evidence that they are benefiting from the process. As the year has progressed, the students have put more time and effort into their new work. They have improved based on feedback from past work. It is rare that a student does not identify areas needing improvement before I do. Students have also become more skilled in discussing their work, their skills, and their needs.

Through the various types of reflection I have attempted with the students, I have found that in all cases the reflection was productive if they were given time to properly reflect, given reassurance to share their thoughts without reproach or ridicule, and given a focus.

> Busy people typically do not engage in reflection. They rarely treat themselves to reflective experiences unless they are given some time, some structure and the expectations to do so. (Killion & Todnem, 1991, p. 15)

Students, too, are busy people. When given the opportunity to reflect, their reflections improved and their work improved. This fact is enough to encourage me to continue to develop this aspect of my program.

I will continue to focus my own and the students' attention on reflection. I believe it will enable each student to better set and attain personal goals. "When we encourage children to think and talk about their learning, we are providing them with valuable insights. We are also giving children opportunities to extend their understanding of their own learning" (Davies et al., 1992, p. 100). Reflection has had a positive effect on the students in all areas of the school program. It seems to empower children to reach their potential.

In the future, I plan to continue with the Think Books, written self-evaluations, videotapes, audiotapes, and transcripts. I will use full class oral reflection earlier in the year to model reflective talk. I will encourage more small group reflection by giving the students specific times to meet with their work groups, with the explicit purpose of reflecting on their work.

I will also continue my involvement in action research. Exploring a question about my own practice has been quite rewarding. I find that I am more reflective about the things that happen in my classroom. I also learn from my observations and carry out changes with greater confidence because I have been observing my students and my practice carefully. Also, I find that action research is never complete: the discoveries I make in the search for an answer to a question always lead me to new questions. My research into the value of reflection has helped me develop a strong belief that reflection is a necessary and powerful component of learning.

REFERENCES

Chambers, A. (1985). *Booktalk: Occasional writing on literature and children*. London: Bodley Head Ltd.

D'Arcy, P. (1989). Making sense—In journals, learning logs, think-books. In D'Arcy (Ed.), *Making sense, Shaping meaning*: Portsmouth, NH: Heinemann.

Davies, A., Cameron, C., Politano, C., & K. Gregory. (1992). *Together is better: Collaborative assessment, evaluation & reporting*. Winnipeg, Manitoba: Peguis.

Killion, J.P. & Todnem, G. (1991). A process for personal theory building, *Educational Leadership, 48*, n.6. 14–16.

Newman, J.M. (1987). Learning to teach by uncovering our assumptions. *Language Arts, 64,* 727–737.

Perkins, D., & Blythe, T. (1994). Putting understanding up front. *Educational Leadership, 51,* 4–7.

Richert, A.E. (1990). Teaching teachers to reflect: A consideration of programme structure. *Journal of Curriculum Studies, 22,* 509–527.

Schon, D.A. (1988). *Educating the reflective practitioner.* San Francisco, CA: Jossey-Bass.

Simmons, R. (1994). The horse before the cart: Assessing for understanding. *Educational Leadership, 51,* 22–23.

LITERATURE CITED

Smucker, B. (1992). *Garth and the mermaid.* Toronto: Viking/Penguin.

CHAPTER 4

Students Telling Stories: Inquiry into the Process of Learning Stories

Judy Caulfield

Caulfield is currently a teacher for the Peel Board of Education and a graduate student pursuing the Doctor of Education at Ontario Institute for Studies in Education in Toronto, Ontario, Canada. Many of her students are first generation Canadians, making oral language and English as a Second Language important parts of the curriculum. With 26 years of teaching experience, Caulfield has been actively involved in storytelling for a decade, telling stories at conferences and festivals as well as in her classroom.

Unless its citizens create a shared body of narratives, a tellingware that includes a nation's many diverse voices, the people of that land will have little power to imagine a common future for themselves. (Yashinsky, 1993, p. 12)

◼ Story has great power in our lives. It has the power to connect us to ourselves and to others. Students who at other times are restless will lean forward and become captivated when told a story. When stories are acknowledged and included within the school culture, a powerful message is sent to students. Celebrating both formal narratives and informal family stories encourages students to take the next step to become storytellers themselves.

What happens when students go from being listeners to being storytellers? What changes occur in their language as they prepare a story to tell it to an audience? What motivates storytellers to sustain their personal engagement in the work in order to learn a story to tell? I have been seeking to learn more about these issues as I work with students on storytelling and as I seek to understand my role in facilitating their learning.

In connection with a study unit on the Caribbean, my class was reading and retelling Anansi stories, which are of African descent. They were brought to the West Indies by African slaves and have flourished and spread to the United States and Canada. Two of my students focused on *Anansi's Old Riding Horse* (Sherlock, 1954). In this story, Anansi (who is a man that changes into a spider when he is in trouble) wants to marry Miss Selina, but Tiger is also courting Miss Selina. In order to discourage Miss Selina from marrying Tiger, Anansi decides to tell her that Tiger is only an old riding horse. When Tiger finds out, he sets out to bring back Anansi to tell the truth. Anansi feigns illness, and through a series of tricks, ends up getting Tiger—looking very much like a riding horse wearing a blanket, with a rope about his neck, and with Anansi carrying a stick for a whip—to carry him to Miss Selina's house.

Collecting Data

To systematically analyze the changes in language during the learning of a story, I taperecorded two students (a grade five and a grade six student) on three occasions as they worked together on learning the story *Anansi's Old Riding-Horse*. First the students heard me tell the story; then they retold it together. We listened to the recording of their telling of the story and discussed their telling and ways that they might want to change it. Then they retold it. Once again we listened to their telling of the story and discussed it. Later, the students heard the story told again and then taperecorded as they retold the story in the first person as if they were Anansi telling about the event. In setting up these three tellings of the story and the discussions, I duplicated some of the experiences that students have as they work on learning a story.

False Starts: Lack of Fluency or an Indication of Language Skill?

At first, when analyzing the transcripts, I counted as false starts all utterances that seemed to interfere with the story flow. For example, the word "um," a phrase repeated while substituting a word for another word in the phrase, and stumbling as in "s - s - Selina" were all counted as false starts. Using this simple analysis, I noted that the number of false starts decreased from the first telling to the second telling and then increased for the third telling. This was one way of looking at fluency in telling, and it made sense to see false starts decrease after a rehearsal and then increase when students changed to a new perspective (the first person) in the third telling.

This kind of analysis, however, did little to give me insight into the students' language use. If they had been striving for a memorized version, then the smoother flow of words might have indicated more command over the memory of the text. However, students have been encouraged to tell the story in their own words and to understand the story well enough to be comfortable changing it as they told it.

Reading about discourse analysis in literature on English as a second language led me to a new understanding of what I had labeled as false starts. When considered in the view of discourse competence, these utterances can be seen as strategies and are effective in maintaining the coherence of the story (Savignon, 1983). Instead of false starts, utterances such as "um" are pause fillers and, as such, allow the speaker a moment to choose the best phrase to use next. "Um" also communicates with the audience, or storytelling partner, that the teller is about to continue. It helps maintain the turn of the speaker, which tells the partner that the speaker is going to continue his or her turn in a moment.

These utterances—coherence enhancers or correctors—can build a high degree of congruity within the story. For example, in the Anansi story retelling the students corrected the character's name and any pronouns so that the male or female identity of the speaker was not confused. Time and place were clarified with the use of these strategies. They were also used to clarify details that help the listener understand the facts in the story. For example, in the first telling, this is how Shantel used a coherence enhancer: "Then that's how everyone found out that—that um—that's why everyone *thought that it was* that Tiger was a riding horse." In using the phrase "found out" and then correcting it to

"thought that it was," Shantel was making clear her interpretation. It is indeed the crux of the story because Anansi wanted everyone to have the *impression* of Tiger as being a riding horse.

The first telling of the story could be seen as a rehearsal—students were at the stage of remembering sequence and details in the story. Pause fillers gave them time to consider what came next. The fact that there were fewer pause fillers in the second telling indicated the success of a rehearsal in developing more confidence and flow of the sequence of the story.

Also to be noted is that after the two students had listened to their first telling, they decided that they wanted to tell with fewer "buts and ands." In their second telling, the students dramatically cut down on their use of inappropriate "ands," starting half as many sentences with the word. The story did not suffer from this focus on word usage; instead, while consciously avoiding overuse of "and," students also developed the story further, told it more fluently and used more expression.

One would expect that the third telling of the story might have fewer or no "ums" at all. Perhaps if the story had been retold the same as the first two times this would be true. The storyline would be more committed to memory in a more consistent use of words and phrases with less need for pauses for remembering what comes next. However, in the third telling of the story, the students shifted to first person by telling the story as if they were Anansi. The difficulty of this task and the concentration of the students is indicated by the increased number of pause fillers. First person requires a change of pronouns, which is a visible sign of the shift. More important are the modifications in point of view and perspective as the story changes as if it were told by Anansi himself.

Elaboration: The Story Grows and Changes as Students Gain Understanding and Depth

With each subsequent telling of the Anansi tale, the students added details and expanded the situations to give a more complete picture of the story. This is evident when comparing the three openings. In the first telling, the students related the basic details of this story. Lorraine said,

> There was once was a tiger who walked on two legs.... Everybody respected him. Monkey always liked to play tricks on people but never on Tiger.

In the second telling, the students were more specific by stating that the setting was the Caribbean jungles. They elaborated by naming each of the secondary figures involved, instead of just saying "the animals," and by explaining why Monkey was hesitant to play tricks on Tiger.

Shantel

This is an Anansi story.

Lorraine

(whispers) Big Lie

Shantel

It's called The Big Lie. In the Caribbean where the jungles were big, there was a tiger who walked on two feet. *Everybody* in the jungle respected him. The cow...peacock... rabbit,

Lorraine

The monkey, especially the monkey. The monkey, 'cause always—the monkey always likes to play tricks on other animals but *never ever* the tiger. And the *only* person that *never* ever liked the tiger was Anansi.

In the third telling switching from third person to first person narrative was a conscious decision to help the students change perspective on the story. Students were moved away from repetition of the story without further insights, and retold the story with fresh understanding and with new demands on their telling.

Lorraine

Okay...when I was living in the jungle with all my friends...I liked *every, every* animal in the jungle and I also loved Miss Selina. But the *one* person I *really* despised was that big tiger. (whispers) go.

Shantel

What do I say?

Teacher

You might start to tell why he despised Tiger. What do you think comes next?

Shantel

Well, why I despised Tiger was because he liked Miss Selina and I liked Miss Selina and I wanted to marry her and so did Tiger.

Lorraine

So I thought of a plan of getting the tiger *out of the way of our relationship.* And everybody was really confused because she was nice to me and now—then she was nice to Tiger so everybody was really confused. But one day, I thought of changing that all.

This telling also elaborated on Anansi's reasons for his trick. Especially effective was Lorraine's phrase "getting the tiger *out of the way of our relationship.*" Lorraine was clearly demonstrating that she felt that Anansi believed Miss Selina to be seriously involved with him. The closing of this part of the third telling was equally effective. After setting the scene and introducing the characters, Lorraine drew upon the curiosity of the listener by hinting at Anansi's plan with the words "But one day, I thought of changing that all."

While the plot stayed the same, the story details did not remain fixed across the three tellings. The story was grow-

ing and changing in the children's minds. The children worked hard to communicate effectively their expanding sense of the story's evolution.

Another part of the story that is useful to compare in the three tellings is when Miss Selina told Tiger that Anansi had said Tiger was just an old riding horse. In the first version, the storyline was bare: "And she did [tell Tiger what Anansi had said] and Tiger was very angry."

In the second version, the circumstances of Tiger finding out about the lie were amplified.

Lorraine

So the next day Selina walked by and found Tiger and she was just *ignoring* him, completely ignoring him! And Tiger wondered why 'cause she always came along and said, "Come over here let me talk to you" or "What would you like talk about?" But she—that day she completely ignored him. So Tiger went up to her and said, "Why aren't you talking to me? Why are you ignoring me as if I don't exist?" "Anansi told me that you're a riding horse...."

By the time the students told the story the third time, they had added an extended conversation between Miss Selina and Tiger.

Shantel

Then, one day, Miss Selina was outside and Tiger came. Miss Selina didn't even say a word, she just walked past him, and Tiger said, "What's going on?"

Lorraine

"You don't have to be surprised," she said. "I already know and everybody else knows that I'm—that you're a rocking horse—"

Shantel

(whispers) riding

Lorraine

...a riding horse." "What?" roared the tiger. "You don't have to be surprised. We can be respectful the same way." "Who told you that?" (And by the way, Tiger really had a temper.) "Well, Anansi told me that you're a riding horse. When he was little he used to ride on you all the time."

Shantel

"Oh wait 'til I get my hands on that Anansi. I'm going to rip him from limb to limb. But first I'm gonna bring him here and let him tell you the *truth*."

The students also included the aside "And by the way, Tiger really had a temper" in this version. This was an understatement, but one that the audience would relish and enjoy, looking forward to examples of Tiger's wrath at the obvious lie. The students went on to give a complete picture of Tiger who "roared" and made colorful threats: "Oh wait 'til I get my hands on that Anansi. I'm going to rip him from limb to limb." Their use of repetition was effective as they had Tiger repeat, "Wait 'til I get that Anan-

si," while he sought out Anansi in the jungle. Repetition emphasized the point and drew in the listener to mentally, if not vocally, speak the line along with the storytellers. Lorraine's description was effective in enabling me to visualize the pathway (with the animals on it) parting before the wrathful Tiger on his way to Anansi.

> *I remember* everybody, *every animal in the jungle clearing the pathway because—because Tiger was coming through and* nobody *bothered to go in his way.*

In both of these segments of the story, it was evident that with further telling of the story, students were able to gain competence in creating a clearer image for the audience. They added details as well as extended and elaborated situations. They also used some sophisticated foreshadowing and created a foreboding mood. The story became richer as they dramatized Tiger's anger. Appreciation of Anansi's trick increased as more of the details were elaborated.

The exercise of the students telling, listening to their telling on the tape-recorder, and setting goals for improving their telling of the story was very effective in this circumstance. Because the students were working toward the goal of telling the story to an audience, authenticity in working on and improving the telling of their story was maintained.

Storytelling in the First Person

When she began telling the story in the first person, Lorraine was accepting a new interpretation of the story. She did not duplicate the opening from the version of the story that she had heard. Instead, she stepped into Anansi's egocentric character, putting the focus on him.

> Okay.... When I was living in the jungle with all my friends. I liked every, every animal in the jungle and I also loved Miss Selina. But the one person I really despised was that big tiger.

This focused the story on Anansi's interpretation of the event in keeping with Anansi's self-centered character. Lorraine's version had Anansi begin with himself because he would always see himself as the focus of events. This was a clear example of Lorraine's understanding of Anansi's character and her ability to apply this knowledge in interpreting a situation. Lorraine ended the story by connecting her telling with other Anansi stories:

> And that's why, because of me, today tigers run on four feet to get away faster. I turned into a spider as usual, and crawled up a tree behind a leaf.

Part of Lorraine and Shantel's knowledge of Anansi's traits was possible because the class had heard many Anansi stories. It is also a reminder that hearing a story is not just a single event but a part of interconnectedness in stories and in our lives.

Lorraine's following interview about storytelling revealed that she had some very clear ideas about what was happening when she was telling in the first person.

Teacher

What's the difference in telling the story as though you are the storyteller—the narrator—or telling it as though you are the character?

Lorraine

It's like you are telling the story, but the character has more experience. Like if you're Anansi you could tell anything. Like what happened or "I went down so and so road and I came to my house and I was very scared. Like—you say their feelings about when they heard Tiger roaring down the road. And the storyteller, they tell good too, but in a way like I said before, you have to experiment— experience. And that's how it feels for me when I say that I'm Anansi or I'm Jack.

Teacher

Mhum. It feels as though you are experiencing the story?

Lorraine

Well it feels as though I am experiencing the person as well.

What a wonderful way of expressing the feeling of being "in role." For

Lorraine, the narrator does not have all the knowledge of the character or of the character's "experiences." Lorraine clarified for me that it was not as though she was experiencing the story, but rather that she was experiencing the person. Lorraine's revelation of experiencing the person suggests the importance for others to work in this mode, for it may help us see the world through another's eyes.

Shantel, as the second teller in this version, was at a disadvantage. Lorraine had begun telling the story and had immediately gone into role as Anansi. She had seen an interesting place to start the story from Anansi's point of view. The two girls had not stopped to discuss how this would evolve. So Shantel, who was not as experienced in first-person telling, was then being asked to retell from a new perspective (and to jump in where someone else had started without consultation). She had a challenge before her. "What should I say?" she asked. My response got her started, but I made the mistake of talking to her as a narrator instead of talking to her as if she were Anansi. "You might start by telling why he despised Tiger. What do you think comes next?" It is a testament to her ability to shift gears that she started with "I" when she began telling.

These two students had to listen carefully to each other and respond to each other's telling in order to maintain coherence in the third telling because they were recreating the story as they went along. Shared telling of the story offered support. The students gave each other cues. Lorraine whispered "me" to Shantel to help repair the first-person perspective during the third telling.

Shantel
> Now, Miss Selina, she *did not marry Tiger*. She *did not marry Anansi*.

Lorraine
> (whispers) me

Shantel
> He did not marry me—She did not marry me.

They also had to help each other with the name "Selina" in each one of the versions. Perhaps this is because there is a student named Selin in the grade two class that they work with as reading buddies.

Visualizing the Story

As a story is told, each listener creates his or her own images. Individual response is affected by past experiences. It is one way that students can make a story their own. Egan (1986), in *Teaching as Story Telling*, makes a strong case for using the child's rich imagination in combination with the child's logical mathematical thinking. Egan has reminded us that young children can visualize events and characters from stories that bear no relationship to the life that child has experienced to date. Storytelling can play a unique role in acknowledging and fostering further development of the child's rich imagination. By removing the barrier of page or illustration between the child and the story, storytelling allows and encourages visualization. Drake (1993) also uses visualization with her university students. She finds that it sets the tone for "clearing the mind, becoming centered, and being open and responsive to new ideas" (p. 11).

When I interviewed Lorraine about how she "saw" the story *Anansi Finds a Fool* (Aardema, 1992), she responded, "Sometimes I picture Dwayne as Anansi and Germane as the Fool. For some reason I do that." Lorraine was personalizing the story by inviting into it her two younger brothers as the two main characters. This ability to see her brothers within the story helped her flesh out the story and know how the characters experienced the story. When she spontaneously connects and interweaves stories with her life experiences Lorraine is demonstrating insightful understanding of the story. As the king says to his storyteller in Yashinsky's (1992) *The Storyteller at Fault*, "The teller and the tale are one and cannot be separated, for each one shelters the other" (p. 60).

I explored with Lorraine how the images that we create for the story might vary from person to person in the following dialogue.

Lorraine

And sometimes I picture it in my own mind. I picture the Caribbean—homeland. Sun. Well, I see it as Jamaica because I have the feeling of the heat. And I mostly see Jamaica because you might see St. Vincent and some people might see the Cuba, but my—in my mind I see Jamaica.

Teacher

If you were to draw what was in your mind and I was to draw what was in my mind, how would the pictures look different?

Lorraine

Well, you'd see a whole difference. It's—when you see my picture you can see the Caribbean. And if some Jamaican guy comes up and sees your picture they'd know right away that it's from another country. And yours would probably be tall buildings and mine would probably be—mmm—Kingston. In a way.

Teacher

All right, you've talked about my tall buildings. Yours would be...give me the comparison. Mine is tall buildings, yours is...

Lorraine

Like sort of in a way palm trees, bumpy road, um, coconut trees — yah.

Lorraine did not include these details in her storytelling of this Anansi story; however, it was quite evident that she had a clear image of the setting of this story and the action as it took place. This is one thing that enabled her to have confidence in telling the story in her own words and communicating it effectively.

The Tools of the Arts

When inquiring into the arts, one must use the tools of the arts—drama, art, and writing. Inquiry into storytelling must not model the traditional method of prose and poetry analysis in which isolated portions were dissected to find out the "real interpretation." The "real interpretation" was usually that of an adult expert—never the student (Swartz, 1993). Students were not deemed to have the knowledge or depth to interpret material. It often became the search for what the teacher wanted students to say about a portion of a text.

Storytelling As Inquiry

How then is my students' work on storytelling an inquiry for them? It is an inquiry as they focus on learning about the story and on understanding the story in depth. Students are inquirers about the connections storytelling has for them and for others. Wells (1994) likens action research to student-directed learning:

> What both have in common is the fundamental premise that understanding grows out of purposeful action and is cumulatively constructed as the learner brings his or her current knowledge to bear on new situations and information in an effort to "make sense" of them. (p. 29)

Learning a story is hard work. In the work of learning a story to tell, students can bring many devices and techniques that will help them get inside the story. They will be building on past life experiences and past experiences with story to see the universal truths that are communicated in the story that they choose to learn. Drama, visualization, drawing, and diagramming the story all help the students make important connections so that they become a part of the story that they will tell. As students learn to tell a story, they have the dual role of getting inside the story and of communicating the story to an audience. Part of their inquiry will be what makes them effective communicators of this story. Given a structure and the expectation (Killion & Todnem, 1991) that *they* hold the key to learning about their chosen stories, students become more confident in manipulating the stories so that they make sense to themselves and to their audience.

Teachers As Researchers: Being Part of a Community

It is important to note that in my storytelling journey of discovery, my colleagues both in my school community and in the university community have been key factors. A significant part of teacher inquiry for me has been the talk about the inquiry. Recently, a colleague from a university class and I were discussing our research. She exclaimed that she had suddenly recognized the common ground that music and storytelling share in understanding about constructed meaning. Music, she explained, is a complex process. To understand what is taking place, the listener is constantly reaching back while also anticipating in order to understand the present. She saw that music and storytelling both involve a sense of time having a multidimensional quality (E. MacDonald, personal communication, 1995). Each time we talk, we both get more excited about the connections and about the avenues of research that are opening for us. Elizabeth helps me by connecting me to a holistic view of storytelling in an educational context. That is what is truly exciting about being an inquirer within a community of inquirers.

As I continue to work with students in storytelling, how will this part of my inquiry unfold? My peers in a graduate university class challenged me to think again about the importance of storytelling. They queried the significance of the data on the three retellings of the Anansi story. My initial focus on the false starts in a telling was a shallow look at the data and would lead me no further into understanding the process. One of my teaching colleagues was enthusiastic about my research into children's storytelling and suggested that I read the English as a second language literature I mentioned earlier. Understanding students' attempts to maintain coherence when talking has shed new light on how I listen to and receive student talk in all areas of my school work. Perhaps I am more patient in listening to my students' pauses and repeats because I realize they form a function and indicate students are refining and clarifying their speech. I hope that I am less likely to dismiss it as poor language. My awareness makes me a better listener and educator as I communicate to students the importance of clarifying language, whether we are talking about stories, science experiments, or math concepts.

Questions from fellow graduate students about whether students created new stories or were just memorizing stories bothered me. Is storytelling only of value in education when students create new stories to tell? Part of my goal in storytelling is to celebrate folk- and fairytales because of their enduring universal qualities. The old stories connect us to our past and our present. This perspective aside, the questions of my students' creative input has spurred me to add new dimensions when I work on a story together with my students. I continue to seek new ways of encouraging them to find their own way of interpreting and telling stories.

Why Storytelling?

Why do I feel that storytelling is a viable and valuable part of a learning environment? What parts of it may be seen to complement active meaning making? Narrative is the natural form we use to make sense of our lives. We use story events to give our lives form and structure—to see them more clearly. By structuring the incidents and the complex relationships in our lives we seek to see patterns and to understand events in a broader context rather than in small fragmented pieces.

Learning to tell stories is not a mindless activity of memorizing the words of a story. When a student retells a story—even when it is retold in much the same manner in which it was heard—he or she is working on grasping and using the structure of story, using effective vocabulary, as well as embellishing or reducing elements of the story as the student comes to express his or her understanding. The student, in using his or her own words, will be constantly striving for and assessing his or her effectiveness. A grade four student once said: "If I'm telling a story I can make up adjustments, and if I forget, I can always add in whatever makes sense."

Harold Rosen reflects on the role of storytelling for the students in Betty Rosen's (1988) book *And None of It Was Nonsense*:

> We should militantly assert that the students in this book are mean-

> ing-makers even when—perhaps especially when—they are retelling. They rework the stories they have heard to make new meanings to shift their view of the world or amplify it. At the same time, they are constructing their own social selves. (p. 167)

For many students, such as English as a second language students or those with weak decoding skills, storytelling bridges the gap between the author and the reader that the written word forces upon them. It confirms and celebrates students' own narrative skills.

Why bother with storytelling? With all this talk of narrative, why not just read to students? My extensive library at home proclaims my love of reading; however, storytelling adds a different and important dimension. As Petersen said 60 years ago: "Language is not an end in itself...it is a way of connection between souls, a means of communication" (cited in Savignon, 1983, p. 48). Storytelling is important because of its essential personal communication.

Continuing the Search to Understand Storytelling

Storytelling is about communities (Barton & Booth, 1990). Although reading is a great delight, it is often a solitary event. Telling stories, either personal or formal, is one of the most powerful social interactions that we experience.

Storytelling, by its very nature, is an interconnecting event; it takes at least two people. We are a society that relies heavily on print. As students progress through the grades, they are expected more and more to respond in writing rather than orally. We must not forget the spoken word with its element of relationships and personal interactions. The ability to communicate and to respond to one another in person is part of the essence of our humanity. It brings us into communities as beings with interactive skills and common stories to bind us together. It is one important facet of personal connection that must not be lost.

The interpersonal communication skills developed by students who tell stories is an essential part of making contact with others. Wilkinson (Wilkinson, Davies, & Berrill, 1990), when discussing the shared experience of stories, says: "through language we establish empathy with others [which] can have a unifying effect for an entire group" (p. 150). Students, through storytelling, learn effectiveness in their language skills and their expressive skills as they tell stories to individuals, a few friends, or a large group. When listeners visualize, they are incorporating a variety of senses to interpret the story. Students, as they work on learning a story, are deepening language skills. They are hearing (and reading) stories that are well structured and then developing skills in using these structures themselves. As they work on a story, students develop techniques for evaluating their performance. They see stories with new vision when they tell them from different perspectives. Indeed their new perspective may be a new insight to the audience as well.

An important part of all this is students' ability and willingness to make connections with their audience—be it only one person. They are taking a risk to share themselves, their learning, and their insights. How do you measure the learning? I am still investigating that. I will be returning to my students and working with them to explore why storytelling makes a difference to them.

REFERENCES

Barton, B., & Booth, D. (1990). *Stories in the classroom: Storytelling, reading aloud and role-playing with children*. Markham, Ontario: Pembroke.

Drake, S. (1993). Imagery as a journey for personal and professional renewal. *Orbit, 23.3*, 11–13.

Egan, K. (1986). *Teaching as story telling: An alternative approach to teaching and curriculum in the elementary school*. London, Ontario: Althouse Press.

Killion, J.P. & Todnem, G.R. (1991). A process for personal theory building. *Education Leadership*, 14–16.

Rosen, B. (1988). *And none of it was nonsense: The power of storytelling in school*. Richmond Hill, Ontario: Scholastic.

Savignon, S. (1983). *Communicative competence: Theory and classroom practice*. Reading, MA: Addison Wesley.

Sherlock, P. (1966). *West Indian folk-tales*, p. 105–111. London: Oxford University Press.

Swartz, L. (1993). *Classroom events through poetry.* Markham, Ontario: Pembroke.

Wells, G. (1994). *Changing schools from within: Creating communities of inquiry.* Toronto: Ontario Institute for Studies in Education Press.

Wilkinson, A., Davies, A., & Berrill, D. (1990). *Spoken English illuminated,* 151–174. Buckingham, UK: Open University Press.

Yashinsky, D. (1992). *The storyteller at fault.* Charlottetown, Prince Edward Island: Ragweed Press.

Yashinsky, D. (1993). Tellingware: A headful of stories. *Storytelling Magazine,* 3.3, p. 11–14.

LITERATURE CITED

Aardema, V. (1992). *Anansi finds a fool: an Ashanti Tale.* New York: Dial.

CHAPTER 5

A Language Experience Approach to Elementary Geometry

Monica McGlynn-Stewart

McGlynn-Stewart is a graduate of The Institute of Child Study at the University of Toronto and has recently completed her Master of Education degree at The Ontario Institute for Studies in Education in Toronto, Ontario, Canada. Her teaching experience includes grades one through five, and her research interests focus on topics across the curriculum as she investigates the possibilities of sociocultural and constructivist approaches to teaching.

■ I have never been happy with my approach to mathematics teaching. Like many other elementary teachers, I felt far more comfortable with language arts instruction. So I decided to finish my master's degree in education and pursue my interest in becoming a better math teacher. Two courses, sociocultural theory and constructivism in math education, became the starting points for an inquiry I conducted into alternative approaches to the teaching of geometry. In addition to learning a great deal through conducting the inquiry, I believe that I enriched the social learning context of the students and teacher that I studied.

This investigation presents one elementary classroom teacher's geometry unit in the light of sociocultural and constructivist theories. I will not go into the theories in detail but will outline some key points that guided my investigation. Through my presence, questions, and presentation of transcripts and videotapes to the children and the teacher, I believe that as a teacher-researcher I contributed to the growth of all the participants in their understanding of the teaching and learning of geometry.

Language and Learning

Much has been written about the importance of children's oral language and experience in the early stages of reading and writing instruction (Cummins, 1985, 1989; Delpit, 1990, 1991; Goodman, 1986; Graves, 1978; Heath, 1983; Newman 1985; Smith, 1978), but little can be found about their importance in mathematics instruction. As mentioned in a previous chapter in this book, many elementary teachers no longer think of language teaching as the direct instruction of a set of rules designed to reproduce an accurate product. Instead, these teachers focus on the language and experience that the children bring to the classroom in an effort to guide them to construct meaning from print; they encourage children to speak and write about their experiences and feelings. These teachers focus on the process of children constructing meaning in an exploratory and experimental mode, rather than focusing on the order in which specific skills are mastered. The teacher's role in this model of instruction is to encourage risk-taking and to give guidance as needed by the child.

Typically, children in this instructional model work collaboratively. However, when faced with mathematics instruction, many of the teachers who have chosen not to use direct instruction in language teaching drop what they consider effective in their language arts program and retreat to the endless drills and memorization exercises of algorithms and formulas. The focus on the knowledge and experience that the child brings to the classroom is lost. Also lost is the possibility of creativity and inventiveness. Language may be fun and fluid and flexible and meaningful, but mathematics is seen to be merely facts and procedures to be memorized. The focus moves from the children back to the teacher as the repository of all knowledge. Mathematics is handed to the children as a complete and hitherto unknown package. The multiple meanings possible in literature become, during math time, one correct answer. The group discussions and collaborative projects of language arts classes become the isolating experience of the mathematics worksheet. This does not need to be the case.

As with language arts classes, children come to mathematics classes with a great deal of knowledge and experience gleaned from everyday life. Children also approach mathematics with the same needs: to explore the concepts in a way that makes sense to them, that is consistent with and a natural extension of their previous knowledge and experience. They need to talk and act through this exploration with their peers and under the guidance of their teacher. They need to construct mathematics for themselves, just as they constructed oral language before they came to school and as they construct written language in their language arts classes. The teacher in the study I will describe in this chapter has managed to use what she knows works in language arts programs in her mathematics program.

Background

The community of the school I studied is located in a middle class city on the outskirts of a large multicultural area. The school is small, consisting only of seven classes including a junior (age four) and senior (age five) kindergarten. Because of the school's size, it is possible for the entire staff to know all the children and for most children to know one another. The teachers change the grades they teach periodically, so many have taught the same children for two or three years. The teachers all believe in the value of children's talk, active involvement in their learning, and developmentally appropriate practice.

The group I studied was a combined grade three and four class. For this geometry unit, the two grades had separate math lessons. I focused on the grade three group. There were five girls and seven boys. Except for two children who joined the school in the past year, the children have been in the school for three to four years. For grades one and two, the children have either had their present teacher or one other teacher with similar philosophy and practice. In fact, the two teachers often planned and taught as a team. Therefore, most of the children have spent their school careers in a small, consistent, child-centered environment. This fact has much to do with the successful meaning making that I observed in the geometry unit. The children are well versed in activities such as brainstorming, group work, sharing results, and recording observations.

The teacher is in her eighth year of teaching. Her teacher training emphasized active learning and child-centered practices, principles she has used throughout her career. Because she has taught most of the children before, she knows their abilities and personalities and is able to plan lessons with these things in mind. She regularly attends workshops, is the coordinator of the student teachers in her school, and is pursuing her master's degree in education.

Sociocultural Theory and Constructivism

I believe that sociocultural theory is a useful tool to analyze the ways in which mathematics instruction may become more like a good language experience program, while keeping with the standards in the National Council of Teachers of Mathematics documents (NCTM, 1989; 1991). In his paper, "A Sociocultural Approach to Mind: Some Theoretical Considerations," Wertsch (1990) identifies three general themes in Vygotsky's sociocultural theory. The first theme is his use of a genetic or developmental model. Vygotsky was concerned with several levels of development—the individual, the immediate social environment, the larger cultural environment, and history as a whole. A person must understand the whole context in order to understand the learning of the individual. As the data illustrate, the teacher in the classroom I studied was very aware of the importance of all levels of development when planning her lessons.

The second general theme that Wertsch identifies in Vygotsky's writing is "the claim that higher mental functioning in the individual has its origins in social activity" (p. 141). Vygotsky believes that everything that is internal was once external and social. It is through joint activity with others that an individual appropriates and transforms the cultural norms and practices of his or her society. The implication for this claim in the classroom is that children need the chance to act on ideas and problems with others in order to construct a social or shared understanding before it can be internalized. Then the children will be able to externalize the understanding and use it for further problem-solving. The data I will describe illustrate the high value the teacher I studied places on joint activity as a problem-solving process through which the children expand on their notion of the mathematical concepts introduced.

Last, Wertsch identifies Vygotsky's theory on the essential role played by tools, "technical tools" and signs, "psychological tools" (p. 141) in human mental functions. For Vygotsky, the ultimate tool is language. The mediating role played by language is of supreme importance in the development of higher mental functions. In the classroom I

investigated, much time and value is given to children's talk and writing as they express their beliefs and ideas and as they analyze and justify the discoveries that are made in the process of joint activity.

In addition to these themes, I have explored Vygotsky's notion of scientific and spontaneous concepts and how they relate to learning and teaching in the zone of proximal development. In his paper "The Development of Scientific Concepts in Childhood," Vygotsky (1987) defines spontaneous concepts as those that develop in the course of a child's everyday interaction in society. They are not systematic or generalized, and they may even be contradictory. Scientific concepts are the result of instruction and are systematic and more abstract. Whereas spontaneous concepts begin with the concrete and move toward the general and abstract, scientific concepts begin with the abstract and move toward the concrete. The two types of concepts move in opposite, but (for the individual) complementary, directions. Throughout development there is a shifting back and forth between the types of concepts that influence one another.

Moreover, the development of scientific concepts consists of "the progressive emergence of conscious awareness of concepts and thought operations" (p. 185). Spontaneous concepts involve neither conscious awareness nor voluntary control and act as mediators between objects and scientific concepts

(p. 223). Scientific concepts can be transferred without training to other domains of concepts (p. 191). In the context of his discussion of these two types of concepts, Vygotsky introduces the zone of proximal development. The lower level of one's zone is set by what one can understand or accomplish on one's own. The upper limit is what one can understand or accomplish with the aid of a teacher or more accomplished peer. The role of the more accomplished person is to demonstrate, ask leading questions, and give initial elements of a solution (p. 209). In this way, instruction can cause further development.

The teacher in this investigation was adept at eliciting the children's spontaneous concepts and using them as mediators to scientific concepts. She did this through affirming their spontaneous concepts and emerging scientific concepts about geometry. She also encouraged the development of the children's scientific concepts by asking leading questions, making observations, and modeling, and through the use of semiotic tools such as natural objects and commercially produced building materials. She began with an attempt to understand the children's existing level of concept development—the lower level of their zone of proximal development—so she could create activities that led them toward a more complex and systematic understanding of the material.

The constructivist theory is relevant to my study because it views mathematics as being constructed by the learner, rather than imparted by the teacher. The constructivist theory also believes that mathematical learning occurs most effectively through guided discovery, meaningful application, and problem-solving rather than imitation or rote learning.

Findings

The Teacher's First Interview

I interviewed the teacher about her objectives for her geometry unit. She wanted the children to see geometry in the natural and man-made world around them and to appreciate both the occupational applications and the wonder of it. She used her knowledge of child development in her planning of the unit:

> I think that in grade three they're really starting to look at what their relationship to their world is. In grade one and two and kindergarten, it's much more related to themselves and their families—just that immediate nucleus—and I'm finding that by grade three they are really extending out into the world.

She also expressed her belief that children need to work with manipulative materials to solve problems related to the topic. She planned to use natural objects such as pine cones and flowers to connect the children's outside world to their school world. She then planned to use commercially prepared manipulative materials such as three-dimensional geometric solids and geometric building sets. In Vygotsky's terms, this is as an attempt to draw on the children's spontaneous concepts while introducing the scientific concepts of more formal geometry. With respect to grouping the children, the teacher said, "Group work is the focus because of the language and the interaction and the sharing, but some individual work occurs as well." She was well versed in the concepts and terminology she wanted the children to learn, and she was open to trying new activities. She was able to link what she was teaching to the more abstract ideas of geometry that the children would face in later years.

The Children's First Interview

I interviewed five children individually. I asked them questions such as "What is geometry?" "What is it for?" "How do you learn it?" All the children recognized the word "geometry" but could only define that it had something to do with math. When I prompted with "shapes," they volunteered names of two-dimensional shapes and could identify these shapes in the room. They recounted experiences with geometry in school including the use of pattern blocks and the recording of shapes in the room into a book. When asked what geometry was for, no student could name a use outside the context of learning math. When prompted, they could think of occupations like teacher and builder. All said that they would learn better with friends because, "they can help you" and "you can figure it out together" and "it's more fun with friends." All said that they would prefer the teacher to show rather than tell them about geometry. All the students agreed that they would learn best if they had shapes to feel. Their ideas and values about learning geometry were surprisingly similar to their teacher's.

Classroom Observations: The First Lesson

The first day's activities began with a group brainstorming session around the question, "What is geometry?" The teacher recorded the children's responses on chart paper, repeating what was said, offering encouragement, and periodically reviewing what had been said. The children then broke into small self-chosen groups to examine the natural objects the teacher had provided (shells, pine cones, flowers, and small rocks). The children were instructed to look at the objects, talk about the shapes they noticed, and report to the group on their findings. The children vigorously debated the shapes and grouped them. They then met as a whole group and added more to their chart on geometry. The additions to the chart show that they gained a better understanding of the concepts and their application to the natural world. A greater number and variety of children participated in this second brainstorming session. Finally, having observed and discussed the role of geometry in nature, the children returned to their small groups to explore commercially prepared three-dimensional geometric solids.

The following is a transcript and close reading of the brainstorming session that began the lesson and the unit. The transcript is long because I believe that it is important to see discourse develop over time, to see ideas being picked up, reinforced, and transformed by the participants. The following is a simple yet powerful example of the co-construction of meaning. In my analysis of the transcripts, I have made use of ongoing discussions with the teacher regarding her motivation for the choices she made. I have also made use of a more formal final interview.

Teacher
> Over the next few days and into next week, we are going to be looking at something called "geometry." See if you can read it with me. Geometry (writing word on chart paper).

Ben
> That's hard!

Teacher
> It's a hard word to spell, or it's hard as in "geometry is hard?"

Ben
> It's hard to spell.

Teacher
> Spelling the word is hard (nodding). If I said to you today, "What is geometry?" What would you tell me?

Ted
> Math

Teacher
> Ted's said it would be math (writing on chart). Who else has an idea of what geometry is?

James
> A type of math.

Teacher
> So should I just leave math, or should I also include "a type of math?"

James
> It doesn't matter.

Teacher
> Which would you prefer?

James
> A type of math.

Teacher
> A type of math (writing).

Josh
> A type of math?

Teacher
> James would like to say it this way. This is a list of our ideas. What else is there? Sabrina?

The teacher's encouragement and nonjudgmental comments set the scene for risk-taking among the students. This begins in the opening interchange with Ben. Rather than telling him that geometry was fun or easy, the teacher asked for clarification of what he felt was "hard" about geometry and then confirmed his feelings about the difficulty of spelling the word. It would have been easy for her to assume that Ben was talking about geometry itself and to negate his feelings in an effort to start off the lesson with a more positive sentiment. In addition to showing that she is patient and open to suggestion, the teacher also shows her interest in accurately understanding and recording the children's ideas. This is demonstrated when she asks James for clarification of how he would like his idea recorded and defends his distinction when Josh questions it.

Here, the transcript continues.

Sabrina

Shapes.

Teacher

Shapes (writing). Sabrina says it's shapes. Think about everything you think you know about geometry. Pretend I don't know anything about it and you are describing it to me.

Carolyn

How you can sort things with geometry.

Teacher

Sort things with geometry (writing). Have you ever done that Carolyn?... Have you ever sorted things with geometry?...that you can remember?

Carolyn

I'm not sure. I can't remember.

Teacher

Not sure. OK.

Sandy

I think we did it in Ms. R.'s class.

Teacher

You think so Sandy?

Lots of voices

Yeah, yeah we did, oh yeah.

Sandy

We looked for circles and squares. We wrote in a book what it was.

Teacher

Did you sort it any other way? Did you sort anything else in Ms. R.'s class?

James

(inaudible)

Once a safe and accepting atmosphere is established, children who do not often speak in whole group discussions jump in. It is interesting to note that Sabrina, Carolyn, and Sandy were students I had interviewed earlier. I believe the early interviews gave these three the chance to rehearse their ideas and gave them the confidence to offer these ideas in a whole group setting, something they rarely did. In this dialogue the teacher appeals to the students' sense of play by asking them to reverse roles and pretend that they are teaching her. This adds to the nonthreatening nature of the exchange. She asked them to take the teacher's perspective, resulting in Carolyn and Sandy remembering teacher-initiated activities from the previous year. This strikes a chord in many children.

In this continuation of dialogue, the teacher reviews the contribution collected so far.

Teacher

(nodding and pointing to the chart) So we've said that it's math. James expanded on that and said that it's a type of math. Someone else said it's shapes, and someone else said that you can sort things with geometry. Any other ideas about what geometry might be or what you could use it for?

Josh

You could use it for building.

Teacher

For building? What would you build?

Ted

I was going to say...

Josh

Towers, skyscrapers, they're all made of squares. If you look at it, it's just one big rectangle, skyscrapers are.

Teacher

(writing) So should I say use it for building or use it for buildings? Or for building buildings?

Ted

Use it for building stuff.

Josh

Building stuff.

Teacher

Use it for building stuff (writing). What's another?

Josh

Use it for everything under the sun.

Teacher

Use it for building (pointing to chart). Is that all right? (she left out the word "stuff") You made another comment—that a building is just one big square. Is that what you said?

Josh

Yeah. Everything is one big, almost everything is one big...is made out of geometry!

Teacher

Really? All right. OK (writing).

Josh

See look! (pointing to the overhead projector) There's a triangle right there! Look! (walking to the projector and outlining a triangular part)

Teacher

So almost everything is made out of geometry (writing).

Ted

(pointing to the overhead) There's a square there, there's a circle there.

Josh

(turning and walking back to the projector at Ted's words) There are four circles and one big square if you look at it (pointing to parts of the projector).

Teacher

Thanks, Josh. (Josh sits down) Can I squeeze this in? (writing) Yes. Almost everything is made of geometry. We might need to examine that a little bit more. I think that's an important point. My "y" is kind of funny (fixing it). Anything else? Yes?

Ted

You learn with it.

Teacher

You learn with it (writing). These are good ideas. Anything else?

James

Shapes can be different sizes.

Ted

We said that already (pointing to chart).

Teacher

All we said was shapes but James is saying all different shapes and sizes. I'm going to do this for "and" (&). It's the short form.

Ted

(quietly) Geometry can be names like circle and square.

Josh

(loudly) Um, um, um, we play with geometry when we play with toy blocks.

Teacher

I'm squeezing them in everywhere because we have so many (referring to items on the chart). Sandy?

Sandy

We find geometry all over the place.

Teacher

We find geometry all over the place (writing). Let's put that one here. You guys have kind of figured out what we're doing this morning and I haven't even told you anything. James?

James

Whenever you make something, you use geometry.

Teacher

So I can include it here with building. Whenever you make something, you use geometry. Good idea. Any more ideas for now or do you want to think about it?

In this section, after reviewing the initial contributions, the teacher introduces the new question of what geometry could be used for. This leads to Josh's big discovery that "almost everything is made out of geometry." Josh and Ted spontaneously tie the ideas they have been talking about with their immediate environment. Josh's comment prompts him to walk over to the projector and point out a triangle; Josh's actions prompt Ted to notice other shapes in the projector; this in turn prompts Josh to return to the projector to point out the shapes Ted mentioned. This is a quick, spontaneous, and meaningful link of mathematical theory and the "real" world. Sandy and James demonstrate that they are thinking along the same lines before Josh and Ted continue in the following dialogue.

Josh

(interrupting instructions) There's tons of geometry in the calendar (pointing).

Teacher

What kind of geometry?

Josh

Squares, squares, no, I should say rectangles.

Teacher

Rectangles.

Ted

The lines (drawn diagonally across each rectangle as the day passes) make triangles.

Teacher

What do they do to make a triangle?

Josh

They cut the square, or the thing, in half and that makes it.

Teacher

So you're seeing geometry everywhere.

Josh has obviously continued to look at the room for other "real-world" examples during the discussion. He interrupts the teacher's instructions to point out the geometry in the calendar. It is interesting that the teacher did not reprimand Josh for interrupting her, nor did she say that they were finished with the brainstorming part of the lesson. She stopped what she was doing and followed Josh's comments leading to Ted's quite sophisticated observation about the bisection of a rectangle making two triangles. Finally, she links the interruption to the overall theme of her lesson: "So you're seeing geometry everywhere."

I believe that the way the teacher conducted the brainstorming session in a safe and encouraging manner contributed to the group's complex notion of geometry. No one child could have produced the range and complexity of ideas. Even the children as a group, working without the encouragement and prompting of the teacher, could not have done it. The teacher working alone, transmitting the content to the children as a passive audience, could not have done it. The students enthusiastically built on previous experience and on one another's comments under the guidance of the teacher in an active construction of meaning. This was a genuinely collaborative process carried out in the students' zone of proximal development. After this dialogue, the teacher commented that the students had exceeded her expectations and that she planned to modify her subsequent lessons accordingly. This lesson is an exciting example of a collaborative and constructive meaning-making process that could not have occurred in a traditional mathematics classroom.

When shown a transcript from this lesson, the teacher was generally pleased at her reflection and extension of the children's ideas, what she called "active listening." However, she was disturbed by the degree to which the boys, particularly Josh, dominated the lesson. She had been aware of it at the time, but the transcript confirmed her feelings. She was glad that she had spent so much time with the girls in the small group session. She continued to think aloud about the best way to handle Josh. This confirmed my belief that, by interviewing the teacher, I was a positive instrument in her ongoing teacher development. Because I had the time and resources to tape, interview, and share comments and transcripts, she was able to reflect and alter her teaching practice.

Later in the morning I took five children to watch the video I had taken of their group working with the natural objects. I asked them to watch the video and tell me what they were doing and what they were learning from their actions. The session was not very fruitful. The children spent much of the time laughing at themselves and making comments about how the video changed the color of things and about how I was not in the picture, although I had been there (behind the camera).

Classroom Observations: Lesson Two

Lesson Two consisted of a circle-building time with a construction material with which one can construct two-dimensional and three-dimensional shapes. This was followed by a circle-sharing time and finally a written reflection in individual math logs. The teacher began by reviewing some of the ideas that had arisen the previous day. She introduced the material, which was new to the children, and instructed them to explore it and make any shapes they liked. She negotiated with the children about where and how to work. She gave them the choice of working in small groups at tables or as a whole group on the rug. They voted and decided to work on the rug as a whole group. This negotiation is an important factor in the

children's ability and willingness to take ownership of their learning.

As the building time went on, the teacher introduced new directions based on what the children were doing, and she drew their attention to the class's constructions and observations. Through using the emerging meaning as a guide and encouraging the children to make predictions, articulate discoveries, and justify conclusions, the teacher was able to learn about her students' existing level of geometric concepts while guiding them toward a more sophisticated level of understanding.

Classroom Observations: Lesson Three

At the beginning of the third lesson, the teacher reviewed the activities and terms that had been part of the previous lessons. She asked the children to tell her all the names of shapes that they knew. In the course of compiling the list on chart paper, she introduced the terms two-dimensional, "flat," and three-dimensional, "popping out." A discussion ensued over whether every three-dimensional shape had to have the word "prism" in its name (for example, "pyramid prism"). After the children had exhausted their repertoire of shape names, the teacher introduced the terms "face," "edge," and "vertex." As the children discussed their understanding of these terms, it became evident that they thought a shape could have only one face, like a person, and that the face was the side that was pointing up. The teacher asked them where they could find out more about these terms. The children volunteered the dictionary, encyclopedia, and their math books. The teacher then asked the children to classify the shapes on the chart as two- or three-dimensional. When she received several incorrect and hesitant answers, she changed her mind and said that they would come back to the task after more time working with the geometric solids. She instructed the children to form small groups, sort the shapes, talk about their characteristics, and consult math books or dictionaries if they were unsure.

Through asking probing questions, asking the students to describe and demonstrate their understanding, and reminding them to refer to the resource material, the teacher was convinced that the class could correctly use the terms face, edge, and vertex. After the second and third lessons, I again took a small group to view a section of videotape from the lesson. The second time there was less giggling and more reflection. The third time they were able to report what they had done, discuss difficulties they had faced and the discoveries they had made, and articulate the feelings they had experienced. Each video-watching session produced a greater amount, variety, and quality of metacognitive response from the children.

The Children's Final Interview

I interviewed the five children I had interviewed before the beginning of the unit to see what they understood of their own learning process. At the beginning of this session, I asked the children if they had learned anything about geometry since the first interview. To my surprise, they all agreed that they had not. I was convinced they had learned a significant amount and set about trying to make them aware of their learning.

I began by asking them to describe various two- and three-dimensional shapes I held up. During this activity, many shapes were correctly identified and described using the terms face, edge, and vertex that had been introduced in earlier lessons. They could correctly explain the difference between a two-dimensional and three-dimensional shape. They voluntarily connected the shapes with life experiences, something the teacher had encouraged earlier. Sabrina said that she remembered the word "vertex" because of an amusement park ride called the "Vortex." Sandy remarked on the similarity of the cylinder to organ pipes. Robert noticed that the pyramid block was just like the pyramids in Egypt; and Carolyn described the cone as a Christmas tree.

After the identification exercise, I challenged them to build certain shapes with the building material. They were all able to build a square-based and triangular-based pyramid and a cube. They proceeded to make other shapes and invent names for them based on the terminology they knew. While they built, they called one another's attention to what their shapes looked like "flat" and what they looked like "popping out" following the teacher's earlier modeling.

Finally, I read the children the curriculum guidelines for geometry in grade three. Upon hearing each item, there was a chorus of voices affirming that they understood it. When I finished, I asked them if they had understood those items before the geometry unit. In contrast to the beginning of this session, they all agreed that they had not understood those concepts before but now did. As Carolyn put it, "Yeah, 'cause last year and the year before we didn't know what 3-D and 2-D was. No one even said it in the class before." Other children jumped in and volunteered that they had learned more shape names and ways of describing shapes in terms of faces, edges, and vertices.

As a result of my final session with the children, their final group interview, the children came to realize the complexity of their learning. At the beginning of this session, they did not realize that they had learned anything in the geometry unit, but at the end of our session they were confident that they had learned a great deal. I believe this happened because of the excellent lessons they had with their teacher, but also because as a researcher, I was able to take the time to demonstrate to them their own learning. To use Vygotskian terminology, they had moved along the continuum from spontaneous to scientific concepts but were not yet consciously aware of their own concepts. They were also aware that I was audiotaping, and sometimes videotaping their lessons and their sessions with me. Each time they had been with me, I had played them parts of the audio- or videotape. I believe this had an impact in the final instance of conscious awareness I witnessed. At the end of this session, as we were preparing to go back to the classroom, Carolyn asked rather impatiently why I was not playing the tape for them. They had come to expect this reflective action.

Conclusion

The teacher's approach throughout the unit is very much in line with sociocultural theory. She begins by considering the social and historical experience of the children. Through her knowledge of child development and of these particular children over the past two years, she was able to build on their previous experience or the lower level of their zone of proximal development in order to plan lessons that would stretch them toward the upper level of their zone. She made the links between their spontaneous concepts and scientific concepts by bringing their natural world into the classroom. She built on this experience with commercially prepared objects and finally linked these with the more abstract concepts. The teacher values social learning activity and therefore promoted group work and group talk during problem-solving. She had wide ranging objectives that included a sense of wonder and appreciation for geometry in addition to strictly curricular, mathematical objectives. This is more likely to promote generalization and transferal of scientific concepts to other domains of thought. She is open to individual learning styles and flexible in her approach, realizing that people take different paths to understanding. Finally, she realizes that she is a learner, too, and is willing to take risks with new approaches and to adapt approaches as she goes along.

The children in this study have all come from programs where problem-solving, the use of manipulatives, and group work are the norm. They have internalized their teacher's belief of working together on problems to learn effectively. One child said that the teacher's role is to help students work things out, like a friend. It would be interesting to ask the same questions of children who have been in a traditional teacher-directed math program where working together is considered cheating. I am sure that they would feel differently about the role of the teacher and of their peers.

My final interview with the teacher illustrated what we have seen in the previous data; the teacher is able to act on her philosophy in a very effective manner. Her ability to articulate her beliefs

clearly is undoubtedly an aid in this endeavor. The interview, video-watching, and transcript-sharing episodes with the teacher and children were enormously helpful to me as a researcher and teacher, and also to the other participants in this geometry unit. As a researcher, I had the luxury of time, distance, and lack of direct responsibility for the students and the lessons. I believe that this luxury, in addition to my mere presence during the geometry unit, allowed me to have a positive effect on the situation.

I provided the opportunity for the teacher and a small group of children to articulate and reflect on their ideas, values, and experiences. According to the participants' own accounts, these reflective experiences altered their perceptions, understanding, and behavior with respect to the teaching and learning of geometry.

Through her lesson design and style of facilitation, which adhere to both sociocultural and constructivist theories, the teacher in this study was able to create, with her students, a culture for learning that is starkly different from that of traditional mathematics classrooms. She builds on her knowledge of the children and of child development and the children's language and previous experience. She incorporates the language and experience of the class as it accumulates throughout the unit. She encourages the children to solve problems together with real objects, talk through their experiences, and share and record observations and discoveries. She accepts their ideas and allows sufficient time for joint exploration, still not content with the students' level of development. Through observations, questions, and relevant activities, she leads the children to higher levels of concept development within their zones of proximal development.

The values, practices, norms, and expectations of this math culture direct the children to construct their knowledge together and take responsibility for their own learning, under the guidance of the teacher. The teacher is a knowledgeable guide who challenges, but who is also a learner willing to negotiate and take risks in the shared discovery of meaning. The outside world is welcomed as an object for discussion, experimentation, and evaluation. Here, there is no sharp divide between spontaneous and scientific concepts. Participants are urged to use each concept to illuminate the other. The children working jointly within this culture transform it for use as a tool in their further learning.

REFERENCES

Cummins, J. (1989). *Empowering minority students.* Sacramento, CA: Santillana.

Delpit, L. (1990). Language diversity and learning. In S. Hynds & D. Rubin (Eds), *Perspectives on talk and learning.* Urbana, IL: National Council of Teachers of English.

Delpit, L. (1991, November). A conversation with Lisa Delpit. *Language Arts, 68,* pp. 17–19.

Goodman, K. (1986). *What's whole in whole language?* Richmond Hill, Ontario: Scholastic.

Graves, D. (1978). *Balance the basics: Let them write.* New York: Ford Foundation.

Heath, S.B. (1983). *Ways with words: Language, life, and work in communities and classrooms.* New York: Cambridge University Press.

National Council of Teachers of Mathematics, Commission on Standards for School Mathematics. (1989). *Curriculum and evaluation standards for school mathematics.* Reston, VA: The Council.

National Council of Teachers of Mathematics, Commission on Professional Standards for Teaching Mathematics. (1991). *Professional standards for teaching mathematics.* Reston, VA: The Council.

Newman, J. (1985). *Whole language: Theory in use.* Portsmouth, NH: Heinemann.

Smith, F. (1978). *Reading.* Cambridge, UK: Cambridge University Press.

Vygotsky, L.S. (1987). The development of scientific concepts in childhood. In R.W. Rieber & A.S. Carton (Eds.), *The collected works of L.S. Vygotsky,* Vol. 1. New York: Plenum.

Wertsch, J.V. (1990). The voice of rationality in a sociocultural approach to mind. In L. Moll, (Ed.), *Vygotsky and education: Instructional implications and applications of sociohistorical psychology.* New York: Cambridge University Press.

CHAPTER 6

Technology and R̶
Knowing Our W̶

St. Pierre-Hirtle has taught both preschool a̶
She is currently completing a doctoral program a̶
preservice teachers at Sam Houston State University in ̶
perienced the value of teacher collaboration at the element̶
ondary level.

■ During Christmas break in 1989 I read Atwell's *In the Middle* (1987). With that encouragement, I began trying to build a meaningful curriculum with a range of opportunities, to help my high school students connect their previous life experiences to the traditional curriculum. This began my theory-building journey toward social constructivism (Shor, 1992). Recently I have begun to use computers to support and mediate those socially negotiated meanings among learners. This chapter focuses on a project on which a colleague and I collaborated to help high school students use computer technology as a tool for mediating their learning. During this project we learned about the power of technolo-

gy for our students, and we learned about the potential for collaborative reflection and inquiry for ourselves.

The Beginnings

I began to wonder about the power of technology as a learning tool when I observed a classroom in which students designed, constructed, and lived in a simulated space habitat for 72 hours. Reading, writing, and speaking were used in all aspects of this project. The students proposed the idea, gained support, promoted and documented the project, and provided long-term evaluation and final reports. This project generated enthusiasm among the students

ers the opportu-
ne essence, the
the matter and then
essary to expand the
kav, 1979, p. 7). The
r than teach technology
crossed traditional discipli-
aries, using whatever skills
epts students needed in math,
writing, technology, science,
ganizational management to
ve their purposes. These teachers
students demonstrated that

> the more time and effort students
> invest in the learning process and
> the more intensely they engage in
> their own education, the greater
> will be their growth and achieve-
> ment, their own satisfaction with
> their educational experience, and
> their persistence in college, and the
> more likely they are to continue
> their learning. (National Institute
> of Education, 1985, p. 17)

I decided I wanted to create that kind
of environment for my students. I wanted to create a classroom community in
which

> literacy is a process of social en-
> gagement, where texts are seen as
> part of a dialogue among people
> with common, competing, or often
> opposing interests. Students must
> learn to negotiate and critique
> these positions to come to their
> own informed stands. As they read

> and write about issues, they create
> their own tentative versions of the
> world. (Gere et al., 1992, p. 188)

As I struggled to work with students
in negotiating this environment, I wondered what texts and writings should
make up a constructivist classroom and
what tools were available to assist students in their journey to understanding.
In my school, a large suburban high
school north of Houston, Texas, the
most modern tools for communication
existed in the vocational education department. Technology was not available
in the language arts department. The
use of technology in language arts was
considered pedagogical heresy, somehow depriving students of the time-hon-
ored practices of writing and revising by
hand as well as the traditional teacher-
centered discussion.

I was aware that computers could
help students compose with speed and
ease and that students could learn to
enjoy this process. I looked at the written documents that the vocational education students produced and was
stunned by the polished quality of the
laser-printed documents. I marveled at
this group of students (who had been
labeled as reluctant learners) as they revised texts composed on a computer
until they were satisfied with the quality
of their final product. This was my goal
in language arts—the capacity for continuous improvement among students
who defined their own concept of quali-

ty. I wanted to stop struggling alone and have my students join in the pursuit of quality in reading, writing, and learning.

Developing the Collaborative Technology Project

I found that the vocational education teachers were receptive to forming new alliances with other disciplines to support project-based work. In collaboration with Pat Gutknecht, a microcomputer teacher, I wrote and received a federal grant that provided my language arts classroom with 6 computers, a printer, various software, a modem for access to the Internet; and networking capability with the technology department and their CD-ROM data. Simultaneously, the school district equipped Pat's microcomputer classroom with 25 computers, 2 printers, software, a modem, and the same network access as my classroom. A Houston-based engineering company supported the project by providing us with software training.

The grant provided an opportunity for partnerships and collaborative teamwork. Students participated in various team-building activities designed to promote communication, problem solving, critical thinking, and mentoring practices. My language arts classes joined forces with microcomputer classes to produce multimedia presentations, personalized children's books, and academic and technical papers. We hoped that students, by participating in cooperative strategies, would enhance skill development, gain valuable organizational skills, find that learning can be empowering and self-directed, and learn that school activities can be equivalent to the life and work of the community.

Initially our students were not sure how to respond within this collaborative environment. First, we combined our students to form project teams. This violated their expectations of traditional academic curriculum organization, and they questioned why they should help one another. For the language arts students, the answer was easy: the technology students had the computer skills they needed to learn. The microcomputer students, however, had a difficult time accepting the benefit of extra writing in their computer class. Our school was divided by strict academic discipline boundaries and, although writing-across-the-curriculum was a stated goal in staff development, students' paradigms had not shifted sufficiently to see this as a benefit. Prior to the grant, the microcomputer class had consisted of skill-based workbook activities performed on outdated computers. We explained to these students that through their participation in this project, the school would receive state-of-the-art equipment that would enhance their training. They reluctantly agreed to collaborate on the first project in writing, designing, and producing a customized holiday book for second grade students from a nearby elementary school.

The Christmas Book Publication

Our students began this book project by generating interview questions to use in their initial meeting with the second graders. We discussed young children's developmental characteristics, looking particularly at interests, verbal ability, motivation, and reading level. We emphasized that this project extended beyond the issues of reading, writing, and technology. This project provided a link for the high school students to a whole community of students with whom they would share learning.

The second graders won the hearts of our students immediately. The high school students interviewed their assigned second graders, gathered data, and discussed and reflected on elementary school interest levels, classroom practices, verbal abilities, and social behaviors. The elementary school librarian supplied us with books about seasonal holiday practices from various cultures. We read these children's books, which provided appropriate literary models. We used the computers to create a graphic organizer, a line drawing of four squares, which helped us record our analysis of the basic elements of a story (character, setting, conflict, and resolution) before we began the process of composing the stories.

Collaborative Learning for Teachers

My colleague Pat taught me how to create a table on the software for the graphic organizer, and I taught her the concept of the four-square graphic organizer and the essential elements of the narrative. This was our first step at crossing academic boundary lines, and it was not lost on our students. They watched us learn from each other and watched us teach technology and literacy practices to our students. We each gained confidence from the other as we traveled these uncharted waters. Through time and practice, we became able to cross the subject boundary lines until we became project teachers, not identifiable by subject.

Pat quickly became an expert in generating easy-to-follow directions for any skill our students needed. What we learned, with astonished pleasure, was that even the most complicated skills were quickly assimilated when they supported the children's book project. Some of our equipment arrived late, so in order to meet the holiday deadline, our students had to use a sophisticated desktop publishing software.

Pat's accessible directions got us through the most complicated processes. We all believed that no software program was too tough to tackle in the context of our project. The students created the books with the desktop publishing software after writing their drafts by hand or with the word processor. Pat showed us how to import graphics and text generated during prewriting analysis. The project teams supported one another with editing circles, and we produced more than 60 original holiday books for the elementary students.

Collaborative Learning for Students

In the language arts classroom, computers became a way of life. I divided each class into five or six cooperative base groups (Johnson & Johnson, 1993). Each base group was situated around a large worktable and was connected to the network, where they worked together for their individual and collective success. I had a computer and a liquid crystal display (LCD) panel at my workstation and a network printer that we all used for output. This room design allowed for the "face-to-face promotive interaction" (Johnson & Johnson, 1993, p. 11), which allowed students to promote one another's learning and success and still cooperatively use the computer to support that success.

Base groups set up operating norms that allowed all members to use the computers. Quite a bit of negotiating went into this process, as some students were very skilled in computer use and others were hesitant and fearful about using computers. We spent a lot of time selling the concept of hands-on learning. The barriers of inexperience and fear gradually dissolved, and the students enjoyed the work using their new skills. They reported that it was easy to learn from their peers in the context of their project work, and at the end of the year they were amazed by their progress in computer skills. Several language arts students who had signed up for the microcomputer class either dropped it, feeling they had mastered the skills taught in the class, or moved to a more advanced technology course.

Individual responsibility and accountability were negotiated in these cooperative groups. Throughout the rest of the year, language arts projects typically involved the reading and preparation of a historical background presentation for the class. Groups read, researched, and prepared slides, which allowed their classmates to get a sense of the social, historical, political, cultural, economic, and religious movements that influenced the literature, art, and music of early America.

Groups would search the Internet to find additional graphics or applications to enhance their presentations. One such software program helped a group give a lively presentation on Puritan cultural practices. I was constantly amazed at how much historical data students remembered and transferred to their literary discussions. The role provided for them by the technology-based presentations and the cooperative structure greatly enhanced their learning.

As facilitator, I gave them content and technical guidance, observed and encouraged the organization and management of the process, and taught and encouraged the social skills that supported those processes. Without this facilitation, "hitchhiking" on the work of others, hiding, or getting lost in the group could easily occur. At first I felt uncomfortable with this role, but reminded myself continually of Glasser's theory that students learn as much as 90 percent more effectively when they teach others (Glasser, 1992). John D. Rockefeller said, "I will pay more for the ability to deal with people than any other ability under the sun" (cited in Johnson & Johnson, 1993, p. 13). These two ideas encouraged me through my transition from a teacher who transmitted information to one who helped students transact with information.

I no longer wanted to be a teacher who practiced what Freire (1993) calls the "banking concept" of education. I was seeking to become a problem-posing educator who, along with my students, sought to construct knowledge and meaning in the "dynamic present" (Freire, 1993, p. 65).

Central to the success of this cooperative model was the development of students' interpersonal and small-group skills. Johnson and Johnson (1993) caution that

> Placing socially unskilled individuals in a group and telling them to cooperate does not guarantee that they are able to do so effectively. We are not born instinctively

knowing how to interact effectively with others. Interpersonal and group skills do not magically appear when they are needed. Persons must be taught the social skills required for high-quality collaboration and be motivated to use them if cooperative groups are to be productive. In order to coordinate efforts to achieve mutual goals, students must (1) get to know and trust each other, (2) communicate accurately and unambiguously, (3) accept and support each other, and (4) resolve conflicts constructively. (p.13)

Encouraging groups to be people centered and to use technology to support content development was definitely a challenge. The students were fascinated with the technology but dubious about trusting one another. It took continuous affirmation of the importance of building trust and communication, and opportunities to develop and apply those skills in nonthreatening ways, for students to feel comfortable in this environment. But they grew comfortable and gave me new ideas for structuring the classroom environment and using technology to accomplish those learning goals.

Benefits and Challenges of Computer Technology

The growth in technology skills, literacy strategies, and cooperative work habits demonstrated during the project astonished and pleased Pat and me. When students reflected on their learning in their portfolios, one student reported

The presentation I feel was most effectively prepared was "The First Harvest." I felt our group understood the topic and presented the information in a useful way. Our group used their journals, discussed, and brainstormed in collaborating on this assignment. We worked together to come up with the information that we thought would be helpful to the class. I also felt that this presentation contained the most thorough content. It gave a lot of valuable information on the topic and helped with the understanding of the reading. The preparation of this presentation differed from the others because I was able to work on the computer and bring my ideas to the screen. I like to take charge so I was able to organize the group and prepare a good presentation. Our team worked together on our presentation effectively, which was the reason for the good presentation. As an individual, I improved the enthusiasm of the group and got the audience involved. Technology influenced our presentation because it made the information neater and more interesting to read. It showed the information on a colorful screen which drew the attention of the audience. Technology gives me an alternative way of communicating my ideas instead of just writing on paper.

In addition, technology supported our classroom procedures and gave students more ownership and responsibility for those procedures. I wrote directions or assignments and saved them to a designated network space my students could access. Students would download the assignment onto their own file and then individually or cooperatively work on the project. After saving it, the students would copy the finished work onto the network so I could access it to review and provide responses.

Through these experiences, I discovered that technology can serve multiple purposes in the classroom. In addition to its support of organizational and procedural issues, it enhanced students' abilities to compose, revise, and edit. My language arts students felt that, as long as their work was saved on a disk, they were never done, and they wanted to continue making changes. I found that setting and holding to deadlines sometimes became problematic as work began to accumulate. However, students felt ownership of their work and felt more comfortable having conferences with me about their work. Students and I were able to review completed work and work in progress on screen. Following these reviews, students occasionally went past my deadlines and worked until they were satisfied with their end product. This negotiated process helped me make the transition from a teacher-centered classroom model to a socially constructed student-centered model.

Another advantage my language arts students discovered in creating collaborative presentations using technology is that they used multiple senses and formats to make dry material interesting, colorful, and appealing. Students worked extra hours finding graphic programs and materials, music, and multimedia sources to creatively improve their presentations. The sense of community generated in the creation of such projects greatly enhanced learning as a transactive process.

Assessment became easier to accomplish as students became part of the process. They extracted pieces of existing work saved on disks to answer assessment questions and create portfolios for a review of their work at the end of each semester. Students were pleased with the appearance of the final product because of the quality of the laser print and the multimedia presentation capability.

My students and I also discovered disadvantages to using computers. Technology sometimes hindered large group discussions. Some students fixated on the computers, and I was frustrated by their shift in focus because I believe the human element is a cornerstone of the classroom experience. In our situation, the base group became the center of students' learning communities, and we had to work hard to achieve a sense of class community for the purpose of seminars and large group discussions. This may have bothered me more than the students, but it was difficult for me to walk away from the sense of community. I do not want to see oral discourse or classroom community devalued or replaced by technology.

We learned that another potentially negative aspect of technology education is the inevitable demand on class time. Learning to use the computers sometimes takes longer than it is worth. We had to learn when to walk away from the computers and do a particular project by hand. These incidents occurred when equipment failed, when students failed to save files properly or lost their disks, or when the network was down. We learned to save files and keep up with our work, but it was and continues to be a learning process that takes discipline. My advice to teachers is that they should be judicious about the time they are willing to devote to technology. I have learned to ask whether technology supports my instructional purposes.

Reflection on the Run

Pat and I had been accustomed to working as individual teachers responsible to our students, our departments' curricular goals, and ourselves. We knew that we would need to collaborate frequently to allow our project to work successfully and that a major part of that collaboration would be planning. We did not realize how important reflection was to the success of our program.

Initially we planned to meet twice a week to plan for a once-a-week activity. Because we were dealing with so many new issues with this collaboration, we soon began meeting every morning for at least 30 minutes and often for the whole 50 minutes we had available in our schedules. After the first collaborative class meeting, we discussed how our students responded to the lesson, what instructional strategies worked well, how well we had met our lesson objectives, and how well those objectives met the intent and spirit of the collaborative grant. The goals that we stated in the grant guided our planning and our reflections: Where did we match up? Where were we not consistent? How do we realign to keep the collaborative spirit alive? How do we encourage our students to buy into collaboration and take responsibility for their learning, the learning of their peers, and the learning of the elementary students? Because these goals stayed foremost in our minds, we forged a truly collaborative team.

Just because we were so determined to follow the intent of the grant did not mean that everything ran smoothly for us; we faced many challenges despite our resolve. Student resistance, misun-derstandings between students, and miscommunication between ourselves were all issues we resolved in reflection time. Each time we met, we asked ourselves how we could best support the intent of the grant. We also eventually asked how we achieve quality in our work. Both Pat and I had attended total quality management (TQM) training, and we used the precepts of quality—teamwork, continuous improvement, and customer delight—to frame our reflections. How do we achieve teamwork? Who is the customer? How can the concept of continuous improvement be woven into our students' consciousness and ours? Who defines quality? Who decides when quality is achieved? How is quality achieved? We posted these questions above our computers, and as we met and reflected we continuously asked ourselves these questions.

Reflecting with the guiding principles for the grant and TQM became such a positive part of our work and our day-to-day existence that we broke long-time traditions at our school: we left our own departments to have lunch with each other once or twice a week. At lunch, we would continue our discussions and reflections. We entered into an all day dialogue, which was a continuous process of reflecting, planning, and practice. This process became a part of our morning routine and lunchtime, hallway, phone, e-mail, and carphone conversations, which were all interwoven with our daily lives and existence.

The discussions that guided our practice became "reflections on the run." These informal and fast-paced reflections helped us run our lives in a much more productive and thoughtful way, and we were able to achieve collaboration and support our students in this same process.

What We Learned

Through this year-long project, Pat and I learned from our students that technology is just an additional way of knowing our world—an alternate way to construct knowledge and a powerful way to communicate that knowledge to others. This project helped me envision how to create authentic learning contexts to support my growing understandings of social constructivism. In these collaborative contexts in which students are creating projects for real audiences, I began to see how learners mediate knowledge within a social context. Just as the role of language in a constructivist environment is to mediate between the learner and the world, the role of collaborative work is to allow learners to mediate for one another. The role of computer technology is to support that mediation, to increase the potential for meaning making by suggesting possibilities that we had never before considered.

In addition, this initial attempt to integrate computer technology into language arts helped me see how teachers can collaborate with colleagues across disciplines, if we make time to reflect on what we think we know and what our students are telling us. Both technology and collaborative reflection can help us build rich learning opportunities as we work together to learn more about our work.

REFERENCES

Atwell, N. (1987). *In the middle: Writing, reading, and learning with adolescents*. Portsmouth, NH: Heinemann.

Freire, P. (1993). *Pedagogy of the oppressed*. New York: Continuum.

Gere, A., Fairbanks, C., Howes, A., Roop, L., & Schaafsma, D. (1992). *Language and reflection: An integrated approach to teaching English*. New York: Macmillan.

Glasser, W. (1992). *The quality school*. New York: HarperCollins.

Johnson, D., & Johnson, R. (1993). *Cooperation in the classroom*. Edina, MN: Interaction.

National Institute of Education. (1984). *Involvement in learning*. Washington, DC: Department of Education.

Shor, I. (1992). *Empowering education*. Chicago, IL: University of Chicago Press.

Zukav, G. (1979). *The dancing wu li masters: An overview of the new physics*. New York: Bantam.

CHAPTER 7

Collaboration, Community, and Communication: Modes of Discourse for Teacher Research

Zoe Donoahue

Donoahue is an elementary teacher in Etobicoke, Ontario, Canada, currently teaching grade 4. As a member of a university-based teacher research group in Toronto, she participates in several research communities—in person, through electronic mail, and through research publications. Her inquiry projects emphasize the complex learning networks that result from collaboration.

■ During one school year I worked with a group of elementary teachers to develop a schoolwide model for teaching spelling. Seven teachers met monthly to establish what we believed about the teaching of spelling and how to create programs that were developmentally appropriate for the children and consistent from grade to grade. This chapter will focus on the ways that communities of inquiry and modes of discourse influenced our work.

The inquiry took place within several communities—the teacher group, a university-based research group to which I belonged, and the classroom community. Two broader communities also had an influence: the educators who have re-searched and written about spelling, and the educators who became the audience for my writing and conference presentations about my research findings.

It soon became apparent that these communities overlapped, linked, and influenced one another. Kowal (1994) refers to an article by Nona Lyons in describing the importance of the "multi-level interaction" between different communities, which is "central to the learning process" (p. 194). What she writes about her own research echoes thoughts about our inquiry:

> *These groups [in her case the students in her graduate class in education and their professor, the student teachers and the author, and*

the student teachers and their students] were not working in isolation. The action research project provided a thread that linked all three groups and established an interdependence between them. (p. 194)

I also found that our inquiry contained a link among several communities. This interdependence enriched our inquiry and caused my own learning to be more powerful and meaningful.

These communities used several different modes of discourse: discussions at monthly meetings, written minutes of these meetings, e-mail messages, transcripts of interviews with teachers and children, and written summaries of the literature about spelling instruction. These oral and written modes of discourse were the tools we used to conduct our inquiry and the methods we used to record and reflect on our actions.

The Communities

I had been on the staff of the school for the past nine years but was on a year's leave when we started this inquiry. One reason for initiating the project was to fulfill my last course requirement—to carry out a classroom-based inquiry—for a Master of Education degree. Working with the teachers on an inquiry of our choice satisfied two agendas: meeting the requirements for an independent study course and giving me an opportu-

nity to continue to work with a dedicated and exemplary group of teachers at my school.

This project was not the first time our staff had focused on a curriculum area. Two years previously we had met biweekly to design a developmental continuum for the teaching of research skills, a model that is currently being implemented and improved on (see Chapter 8). The teachers were immediately enthusiastic when I approached them about looking at spelling in a similar way. Spelling is an area about which we had talked, read and debated for years, yet we were not completely satisfied with our spelling programs. We had all read current books and articles about spelling but did not feel that we had integrated these ideas into our teaching. As a result, we decided to carry out a more systematic investigation.

The Classroom Community

The school is a small elementary school of about 180 students ranging from junior kindergarten to grade five. It is located in an urban community in a large metropolitan area. The school population and the teaching staff have been stable from year to year.

Improving programs to benefit the children's learning was the focus of our efforts, so we felt it would be important to hear the children's voices. We were interested in their self-concepts as spellers, their views about spelling instruction, how they approach spelling, how they see spelling in the context of reading and writing, and how their parents work with them on spelling at home. The teacher group worked together to design a set of interview questions that covered these topics. The children's responses would give us ideas about how we could foster positive attitudes and values about spelling, what aspects of programming we needed to evaluate, how the children were internalizing what we were teaching them, how well we were putting spelling in its proper context, and how we could support parents in helping their children at home.

I conducted interviews at the beginning and middle of the project. Children who were identified as working at, below, and above grade level were selected by the teachers, one from each grade. The teachers tried to choose children who would be talkative when interviewed.

I was also interested in the teachers' feelings about being involved with the project. Midway through the year I asked them to discuss, orally or in writing, how the project was affecting their teaching and whether it was making them more reflective. I also asked the teachers to discuss how they felt about the structure and content of our meetings and future directions they would like to see us take. Their responses provided me with important feedback and provided us with ideas that we might pursue together.

The Teacher Community

The seven teachers in the group were classroom teachers of grade one, grade one and two, grade two and three, and grade three and four; a teacher who worked with children with learning disabilities; a teacher librarian who also taught ESL; and the author, who most recently taught grade four and five. The school culture was open and collaborative, and constructive conversations about teaching philosophy, practices, and the children occurred daily.

The University Research Community

During this project I belonged to a university-based group of teacher researchers consisting of five classroom teachers, three teacher educators, and a research officer. This year marked the beginning of a three-year project of teacher inquiries that focused on the role of discourse in the classroom. People's inquiries evolved from their own interests and questions and thus covered a wide range of curriculum areas. We met monthly to discuss our inquiries and plan conference presentations and writing projects. As well, we communicated almost daily on an e-mail network.

The Community of Researchers and Writers About Spelling

Books and articles about spelling were an important part of our inquiry.

One of my commitments as the group leader was to read and share this information in a way that would be useful to the teachers in their work. Many of us had read the same books and articles and attended workshops and presentations, but we had not managed to integrate the ideas into our classroom programs. By giving the teachers ideas from the literature during the project, I hoped that they might be more likely to try them in their classroom programs.

The Broader Community of Educators

Included in an inquiry should be an audience with whom researchers can share their findings. There are many teachers taking courses who conduct classroom research, write papers and make presentations to their classmates, yet their work is never shared with the broader community of educators. This is unfortunate because there is a large potential audience who would be interested in and inspired by hearing about what their colleagues have learned.

Writing about and presenting my inquiry forced me to organize, reflect on, and make sense of what I learned. Knowing that an audience—a real one at a conference or an imagined one as I write—would need to understand my discoveries, caused me to take a closer look at my findings. I would not have done such a close inspection had I been reflecting and writing for my own purposes only.

Modes of Discourse

Monthly Meetings

The teacher group and research group met once a month. The teachers discussed philosophy, children's developmental levels in spelling, assessment, classroom practices, and programming ideas. We debated, asked and answered our questions, reflected on readings, and consequently made changes in classroom programs. We felt that working collaboratively over a whole year and participating in ongoing dialogue at meetings was a powerful way to work. This was far more effective than traditional models of inservice, courses, or reading, because we reflected and made programming changes on our own.

Minutes of Teacher Meetings

The teacher meetings were audiotaped. Each month I used these tapes to write a detailed, running account of what we discussed. These minutes served several purposes. They provided the teachers and me with a complete record of our conversations and helped me choose a direction for the following meeting. By sending out the minutes by e-mail, the research group was updated on our inquiry.

E-Mail

The e-mail network was an important mode of discourse for the research group and had an impact on the whole inquiry. Many interesting conversations about spelling emerged on the e-mail network after I sent out the minutes from the teacher meetings each month.

Transcripts of Interviews

The transcripts of interviews with the teachers and the children demonstrated the effectiveness of the project; they showed how the teachers felt about our work and how effective our work was for the children's learning. Interviewing during the project helped me evaluate our achievements and determine our direction for the second half of the year.

The teachers were interested to read the transcripts of the children's interviews, and they were able to learn a great deal about the children's learning. In the past I found it fascinating to read, word for word, what my students had said to an interviewer who was removed from the classroom. I think children sense that the interviewer is genuinely interested in what they have to say. They do not feel the need to censor their answers as they would for their teacher.

One of Susan's grade three students saw his name on the transcript of his interview. He demanded to know what it was, so they sat down together to read it. When Susan reported this incident in one of our meetings we realized how

powerful sharing the transcripts with the children could be. After reading their transcripts, students might want to add to or clarify their comments and might gain insight about themselves as learners.

Summaries of Literature

The final mode of discourse was the written summaries of the literature on spelling that I compiled for the teachers. These summaries were distributed at meetings or sent to the teachers.

The Link Between the Classroom and the Teacher Communities

The transcriptions of the interviews with the children had an impact on the work of the teacher group. The children's responses affirmed teaching practices, had an influence on classroom programs, and let the teachers know the children's feelings about new programming practices. These responses also helped determine the direction of our inquiry.

The questions that most affirmed teaching practices were those that dealt with attitudes. We were curious how the children perceived themselves as spellers so we asked the question "Are you a speller?" No one answered "no" and one grade two child said "yes." The remaining students said "kind of" because they did not know how to spell everything, but saw improvement in their learning of spelling. Amanda, in grade four, expressed a typical response: "I don't think I'm good and I'm not bad—I'm not perfect so I just do my best and write what I can write." The teachers' interpretation of these responses was that they had been successful at supporting the children's spelling learning and that their programs were meeting their needs.

A second attitude related question was "How do you feel when the teacher says it's time to do spelling?" All children said they liked spelling because they learned to spell new words. Many of the younger children associated spelling time with writing time, which they enjoyed. It was encouraging for the teachers to receive such positive responses to these questions.

The children's responses also helped determine the direction of our inquiry and discussion topics at our meetings. For example, the children were asked how their parents felt about their spelling development and how the parents helped their children at home. None of the children said that their parents were unhappy with the children's progress in spelling. The teachers were pleased because this indicated that parents were beginning to accept and understand how children learn to spell and the relationship to the approximate spelling that was used in our writing programs. Chris expressed it best in the following dialogue with me:

Zoe

What do your parents think of your spelling?

Chris

Good.

Zoe

Why? Why do they think it's good?

Chris

'Cause I'm their kid!

However, we felt that the older children's accounts of how their parents helped them at home conflicted with classroom programs and were probably more in line with the way the parents were taught to spell when they were young. Here are Amanda's and Alexandra's accounts:

Zoe

How do you study weekly list words?

Amanda

Um, we usually bring them home, open the book to the page and um, first look at the spelling, first look at the word and spell, then look another way and try to spell and see if you were right.

Zoe

Okay. Anything else you do to learn the words?

Amanda

Um, you could get your parents to get a piece of paper and a pen and ask you your words and you try to spell them and then write it down.

Zoe

And how do you learn them? What do you do to learn those words?

Alexandra

My mom takes me home, she gives me a piece of paper in front of me, a pen and she calls my words out. If I get them all right I get to watch TV for another half hour and if I'm wrong I have to write them out ten times.

The teachers were discouraged that children were not working with their spelling words at home in ways they had been taught at school. This alerted the teachers that they needed to educate parents as to how they could help their children with spelling. They also needed to encourage the children to tell their parents about the games and activities they did in the classroom. In response, the teachers and I decided to write a pamphlet for parents that detailed our philosophy for spelling instruction, classroom practices for the primary (junior kindergarten to grade two) and junior (grades three to five) divisions, and specific suggestions for parents.

The children's interview responses also influenced classroom programs by letting the teachers know what areas needed more attention. An example came from children's responses to the question of what strategies they used to attempt to spell words and what tricks they used for remembering spellings. Sounding out was the only strategy mentioned, and it was mentioned by every child. Only David could express a trick he uses:

Like if a word rhymes with another word, they'll usually have the same words, I mean letters inside of it. If you know how to spell the other word then you do the same.

The teachers were not surprised by sounding out being the predominant strategy, but they now realized the need to focus on and encourage children to share strategies and tricks they used. Another possibility raised during a meeting was that children might have been using other tricks and strategies but were unaware of and unable to articulate them. Classroom discussions might bring children's thinking to a more conscious level.

A final way that the children's interview responses influenced the teacher group was by giving feedback on new programming practices. Newman (1987) writes about how important it is for teachers to question their beliefs and assumptions; an important part of this is to see how their students interpret the classroom program. Flavia, the grade three and four teacher, had started a system of spelling helpers, a group of six children who would dictate personal spelling lists to four or five children each week. All three children in grade four made positive comments that showed an understanding of the rationale behind this new practice:

Zoe

Would you like it better if the teacher was doing the dictating or do you like it that the kids do it?

Nicole

Well it doesn't really matter. It will be a lot harder for the teacher 'cause there's so many kids. There's usually seven spelling helpers.

Alexandra

Well, it's sort of easier. The kids say it in a better voice like you say it.

Amanda

Um, there's really not much of a difference because they're both asking you your words and you're really just concentrating on your spelling words and listening to the words they say.

Zoe

Why do you think Mrs. Churchill's doing it this way, having the kids do it?

Amanda

Because, get the kids to learn, to ask them how, like to get them to learn how to ask people stuff and um other stuff like that.

The children's interview responses were a wonderful resource for the teacher group in structuring and directing our inquiry.

The Link Between the Teacher Group and the University Research Communities

An interesting and unanticipated link developed between the teacher group and the university-based research group when I sent the monthly minutes from the teacher group's meetings over the e-mail network to university research group members. I expected group members to read them, if only quickly, and familiarize themselves with our project, but I did not expect the supportive and thoughtful responses and the kind of overlapping dialogue that occurred. Following is an analysis of the ways e-mail was used as a result of the sharing of the school-based group's minutes.

1. To affirm beliefs and classroom practices detailed in the minutes:

   Thanks for giving us the notes from your spelling meeting. I found myself nodding in agreement with many of the observations made by your primary and junior teachers. Their observations certainly resonated with my experiences in the primary and junior divisions.

   — *Karen Hume, e-mail communication, Nov. 27, 1994*

2. To report on their own classroom spelling programs:

   In grade two, I do a lot of patterns and word families as my approach to spelling. I also use a program developed by two educators in British Columbia, the McCrackens. It has lots of ideas for beginning spellers. My grade ones do a daily spelling program that takes about 10 minutes that is based on their ideas.

   — *Mary Ann Gianotti, e-mail communication, Nov. 28, 1994*

3. To share classroom practices that link with what was discussed in the minutes:

The reading resource teacher uses a system with unifix cubes of two different colors. The children "build" the word they are trying to learn, one color for vowels and another for consonants. It really seems to make a difference for some kids.

— Monica McGlynn-Stewart, e-mail communication, Nov. 27, 1994

4. To share resources:

I'll certainly be doing a more extensive literature search, but an immediate response to Gordon's question about whether there are books about language history for kids is a definite yes. I collect such books, and can rhyme off five that were most immediately at hand: [five were listed]

— Karen Hume, e-mail communication, Dec. 13, 1994

5. To reflect on their own spelling learning:

For me spelling is a very visual activity. I can look at a word and tell whether it "looks" right or not. Also I like to remember spelling, where appropriate, based on the word's etymology or history.

— Myriam Shechter, e-mail communication, Nov. 27, 1994

6. To seek out answers to my questions:

I was wondering about interviewing the teachers orally or in writing, and I asked the university research group for their opinions. My meeting was the next day, yet I received 4 responses in under 24 hours. I appreciated the immediacy of the network, as well as people's commitment to supporting one another. The following is one response:

I agree with Karen's and Myriam's points, so offering a choice or combining both, as Myriam suggests, may be a good solution. But I also think you will get different information from the two methods. Writing takes much longer than speaking and is typically more reflective. Rather simplistically put, writing is likely to yield depth and speaking breadth.

— Gordon Wells, e-mail communication, Jan. 10, 1995

7. To respond to programming ideas:

The preceding points all detail the connections that the research group community was making with the content being discussed in the teacher community. However, an incident where Patrick, from the university research group, responded directly to something Flavia, from the school-based group, had said (as recorded in the minutes) really emphasized how closely the two communities were interacting:

> *I was interested in Flavia's observation that some people need more direct teaching. Bearing this in mind, perhaps we could also compile a list of useful memory tricks or basic rules. That well-known rule "i before e except after c" is something I have depended on throughout my adult life.*
>
> — Patrick Allen, e-mail communication, Dec. 12, 1994

8. To make suggestions about the direction of our inquiry:

The following is another excerpt from the same message that illustrates how intertwined the two communities were becoming. After sitting in on one of our teacher meetings, Patrick made suggestions as to how the teacher group might proceed with the inquiry.

> *I wondered whether teachers' autobiographies might be a possible source of insight into spelling problems and how to deal with them. Would it be helpful to compile a list of words which we still have difficulty in spelling, and reflect on what causes the problem?*
>
> — Patrick Allen, e-mail communication, Dec. 12, 1994

Another interesting result of the postings was that the university research group members carried on e-mail conversations about their spelling teaching that were independent of me. I found it intriguing that my work with the teachers at school was causing people in the research group to examine their classroom practices and communicate among themselves about similar issues.

The Link Between the Author and Teacher Communities

Over the years the teachers and I had read much of the same literature about spelling. I reread this literature and some newer resources and passed on summaries that I hoped would be interesting and useful to the teachers. The ideas from the community of writers and researchers about spelling were important in our inquiry because they provided a common base of theoretical and practical knowledge on which to draw.

Reading and discussing what others had written helped our group establish beliefs and philosophies about the teaching of spelling. Strickland (1988) writes that teachers who participate in classroom inquiry are aware of questions to which they need answers. Teachers are more likely to be aware of what others have written about a topic and are able to link that knowledge to what they believe. In every meeting at least one person made reference to something they had read. Grounding our work in this community of writers gave validity and a theoretical and research base to our project. When discussing an issue, such as designing spelling lists, teachers were able to relate their own experiences and to refer to what an author had written. For example, during our meetings, we had shared ideas from *Spelling Instruction That Makes Sense* (Phenix & Scott-Dunne, 1991) about giving children lists of words that link together in some way. In her interview, Susan, the grade two and three teacher, wrote about how these ideas affected her program:

> *The child may be studying only two or three word families each week but they discover that because of this they can spell many words. Close to the end of each week, I often ask the child to spell a word that is part of the word family that was studied but the word I choose does not actually appear on the child's list. The child is often surprised and excited to realize that he or she can actually spell this new word based on the spelling work that has been completed that week.*

We constantly debated and examined what we were reading, made links to our own programs, and revised our ideas and our classroom practices. Our inquiry was richer due to our "interactions" with this community of writers and researchers.

The Link Between the Classroom and the University Research Communities

An interesting link developed between the children and the research group after I sent the transcripts of the children's interviews to the research group by e-mail. A recent set of minutes had addressed the issue of how children whose first language is not English learn to spell in their second language. This, combined with the interview transcripts, caused Myriam, the research officer in the research group, to think about a topic in which she was interested. She sent messages to me that showed how the interviews served as a starting point for her own plans and ideas:

> *There are two topics of personal interest that I would like to discuss with children during future interviews... One of them is spelling (you inspired me!), with the emphasis on the linguistic aspect: whether there are different spelling patterns or problems according to the linguistic background of the children. In other words, do children encounter different problems, or do they use different strategies based on their native language? I would appreciate it if you have any ideas in this direction that you can share with me, or specific spelling items that you think might be good to look at in this context— even comparing how your children*

looked at some spelling problem and parallel this with the approach of non-native speakers of English.

— Myriam Shechter, e-mail correspondence, March 21, 1995

The link between the classroom and the university research communities was unexpected, but held exciting possibilities. It was gratifying and affirming to find that another research group member shared my interest in spelling and was influenced by the teachers' work.

Looking Ahead

Teacher research often begins with one teacher working alone with his or her students, but its full power and influence is not felt until the community is extended beyond the classroom walls. This can happen in several ways.

Over the year I made some tentative suggestions to the teachers in our group, thinking that they might like to embark on their own inquiries. I emphasized that they needed only to start with a question they had about their own programs. A couple of teachers expressed some interest in this during our mid-project interviews. My hope for the next school year was that some of them would be interested in conducting their own classroom inquiries and meeting as a group once a month to discuss them.

A second way that the influence of teacher research can be broadened is when teachers share their findings by

publishing their writing and presenting at conferences. Atwell (1989) writes about four kinds of thoughtfulness that are a part of the work of teacher researchers, and her third point deals specifically with joining the community of writers. She stresses that "teacher research informs not only the individual teacher and his or her students, but also the many educators who read scholarly publications and attend professional conferences. As thoughtful practitioners we assume responsibility for the most difficult thinking of all: that required by writing" (p.11). She emphasizes that we must be aware of what others have researched and written about so that we can contribute to this work.

Sharing findings can help get others involved in teacher research. A friend who has started to do her own research this year came to see my presentation at a research conference. She told me that watching me made her feel that she, too, could present at a conference. I have read collections of teacher research and felt that I could contribute a chapter to a similar book. Reading about or listening to someone talk about his or her research can give other teachers the confidence and inspiration to begin their own inquiries or to share their findings with a broader audience.

Revisiting Modes of Discourse

The various modes of discourse were an important part of our inquiry. Not only were they the tools we used to conduct our inquiry and the methods we used to record and reflect on our actions, but they also facilitated the links between the communities, which made the inquiry richer and more meaningful.

Particular modes of inquiry were appropriate and important for particular communities, and the monthly meetings were essential for both the teacher group and research group. Our teacher group meetings were the times when we discussed our philosophies about spelling instruction and how we might put our beliefs into practice. By talking, we established a common vision of spelling programming for grades one to four. As well as meeting face to face, I communicated with the group in writing by giving them the minutes, interview transcripts, and summaries of literature. This written communication about what we talked about, what the children said, and what the literature said was important because it provided a permanent record that could be read and reflected on. A growing collection of written documents was evidence of the work we had done and what we had accomplished.

These written records were shared with the research group as a way of keeping them up to date about our inquiry. The research group's monthly meetings did not often allow time for discussion about people's individual inquiries (although we are planning to provide more time for this next year), and this was the most effective way to keep

people informed. This sharing of information generated a great deal of thought and dialogue about spelling among the members of the research group.

Along with monthly meetings, e-mail was a powerful mode of discourse for the research group, as mentioned. Group members got to know one another more quickly through e-mail than was possible meeting only once a month. We were able to write often, but at times that were convenient for each person. People could share something that happened to them that day, get reactions, and ask for feedback and advice. We all had a chance to respond to a message, which would not always happen at a face-to-face meeting. Articulating our thoughts in writing may have caused us to be more organized and reflective because we had time to think about what we wrote.

In retrospect, I am sure that the teacher group's work would have benefited greatly had its members also been communicating by e-mail. I suspect that there would have been more discussion and reflection about the practices teachers were trying each day in their classrooms, and that the knowledge about one another's teaching would have been brought to discussions at our monthly meetings.

Both oral and written modes of discourse played an important role in our inquiry. Our work and the connections between communities were enriched and strengthened due to the ways that we communicated, recorded, and reflected on what we were doing.

The Strength of Collaboration and Communities

I believe that a group of teachers working together on a common area of interest can have a tremendous impact on classroom programs when there is ongoing dialogue, reading, and a sustained focus on one topic. Wells (1994) writes about teacher collaboration as a crucial component of teacher research, as teachers can support one another and "meet with colleagues to make sense of the research experience by talking it over with others who understand it first hand" (p. 33). He continues,

For this reason, the ideal situation is where a whole school staff, or a majority of its members, together plan and undertake inquiries in relation to an agreed theme, such as the place of writing in the curriculum or the different ways in which talk about books can be encouraged. In addition to the increased collegiality that is created among the staff through engaging in such a meaningful joint activity, the discoveries about learning and teaching made and shared within the group of teacher-researchers can contribute significantly to curriculum policy-making within the school in a way that goes far be-

yond the specific topics to which the inquiries were directed. (p. 33)

One of the main strengths of our inquiry was the commitment of the teachers to learning more about our shared interest and their willingness to discuss their programs and ideas in order to build a collaborative understanding of spelling.

Richardson (1994) writes about collaborative inquiry as an effective type of staff development. Her description fits our project:

Reflective staff development is a type of action research in which a group of teachers examine their beliefs about the teaching of a particular subject, test their assumptions by collecting data on their students, examine their own practices as well as those of their students, and experiment with new practices in their classrooms. (p. 191)

However, a difference in Richardson's description is that she feels that teachers may have a difficult time initiating such projects; she suggests that an outside facilitator provide motivation and structure for the group. I do not believe that this is necessary. In our case, the facilitator was a peer—a teacher on leave from classroom teaching, not a "university or outside expert" who needs to ensure that teachers feel "equality in participation" (p. 191). This arrangement worked well for us, as the teachers took responsibility at meetings for initiating and sustaining discussions and were self-motivated to learn about spelling and to examine and change their teaching practices. I believe that a full-time teacher could also be an effective group leader, although group members might share the job of reading and making notes on the literature.

Elementary classroom teachers teach most, if not all, subjects. I imagine that my feelings of never being able to teach every subject as well as I would like are shared with others. Being involved with action research on one curriculum area can help teachers to focus on that area and feel that they are improving their teaching and their students' learning. Susan's comments illustrate this point:

> *Although I have always been concerned about spelling and have been eager to find effective ways of helping the learners acquire spelling skills, being part of this study has helped me to give the instruction of spelling a higher priority in my classroom program. I am dedicating more time each day to spelling, and the children appear to be enjoying spelling and taking a greater interest in it than they ever have before.*

Strickland (1988) agrees that classroom inquiry "may be one of the very best ways to encourage teacher self-confidence and feelings of empowerment" (pp. 762–763).

An advantage of conducting action research is the opportunity to focus on a specific curriculum area for a prolonged period of time. A common complaint among teachers is how unlikely it is that a one-time inservice session or meeting will have a lasting impact on classroom programs. By contrast, change seems almost inevitable when a group of teachers is committed to finding answers to its questions and working on one curriculum area during the school year. Richardson (1994, p. 192) summarizes four features that are part of successful staff development programs. These features reflect many of the issues discussed in the preceding paragraphs:

1. *The programs should be content-specific; thus the school is seen as the important unit of change.*

2. *Teachers and administrators in a school should be involved in all aspects of the process.*

3. *The process should take place over an extended period of time.*

4. *The content should incorporate current and verified knowledge.*

In addition, ongoing collaborative research allows ample time for reflection, something that teachers know is valuable but may not happen when they are trying to work on many areas of their program. In her interview, Flavia writes about reflection and the power of inquiry as professional development:

I have been more reflective about my practice. This is due to the fact that our discussions have forced me to focus on the issue of spelling. Since we meet regularly and discuss the issues involved in spelling, you can't help but become more reflective about practice. I don't view these meetings as something you go to, talk about something for an hour, and then forget about it. I like this sort of professional development. It really focuses on the needs of the school, the teachers, and the student population. Teachers making decisions about their own professional needs in order to benefit students.

In their interviews, I asked the teachers to think about how the project influenced their teaching. The following are responses, first from Caryl, then from Dianne:

I suppose it would be confirming what I'm doing. It has caused me to pay more attention over the course of the year to anything I've come across that has to do with spelling. So I've definitely paid attention to any little documents I've come across, or articles, or the odd book I've come across that has to do with spelling, I've looked at it a little more closely than I might otherwise have looked at it. So in that way it's had an impact on me.

First of all, for me personally, it confirmed a lot of the things I was doing because spelling's been such an issue for me for the last three or four years. And ever since I've been working with you we've been talking about it. When I first started teaching grade one I wasn't good at—even when the kids were ready—giving them more formalized spelling. I was a little bit afraid to do that. So I think that in combination with getting together with this group and reading convinced me that that was the best thing to do for those kids.

In the end, the project took on meaning beyond my original goal of working with the teachers on spelling. The insights and discoveries about how the communities interacted and affected one another were very powerful. The examination of the modes of discourse that fueled these links increased my understanding of how an inquiry can be affected by the ways people communicate. Collaboration, communication, and community were central to the effectiveness of our inquiry.

REFERENCES

Atwell, N. (1989, Spring). The thoughtful practitioner. *Teachers networking: The whole language newsletter*, 9–12.

Kowal, M. (1994). Who teaches the teachers?: Community, collaboration and conversation in the learning process. In G. Wells (Ed.), *Changing schools from within* (pp. 171–

195). Toronto: Ontario Institute for Studies in Education Press.

Newman, J. (1987). Learning to teach by uncovering our assumptions. *Language Arts, 64*, 727–737.

Phenix, J,. & Scott-Dunne, D. (1991). *Spelling instruction that makes sense*. Markham, Ontario: Pembroke.

Richardson, V. (1994). Teacher inquiry as professional development. In S. Hollingsworth &
H. Sockett (Eds.), *Teacher Research and Educational Reform* (pp. 186–203). Chicago: University of Chicago Press.

Strickland, D.S. (1988). The teacher as researcher: Toward the extended professional. *Language Arts, 65*, 754–764.

Wells, G. (1994). Introduction. In G. Wells (Ed.), *Changing schools from within* (pp. 1–35). Toronto: Ontario Institute for Studies in Education Press.

CHAPTER 8

Collaborative Inquiry: The Practice of Professional Development

Flavia Churchill

Churchill has taught for 10 years in the province of Ontario, Canada, teaching all grades from 1 to 4, as well as in special education classes. She is currently working on her Master of Education degree at York University, Ontario. She has sustained collaborative inquiry for several years, and suggests that long term collaboration is not only possible, but essential to meaningful school reform.

■ Teacher leadership and the professional development of teachers is viewed as essential if quality learning for all is to be achieved (Fullan, 1994). Fullan states "A wholesale transformation of the teaching profession is necessary. Teacher leadership is not for a few; it is for all" (p. 246). This chapter will describe a collaborative inquiry that occurred at one elementary school. This collaborative inquiry was driven by a teacher leadership shared by all members of the group.

Collaborative inquiry is a form of professional development that can lead to powerful reforms within schools. Collaboration, or collegiality, is a term that Little (Sparks, 1994) reserves for the joint work on the problems of teaching.

Fullan (1994) states that "today's teachers must be committed to, skilled at, and involved in collaborative work cultures inside and outside of the school" (p. 246). In 1991, a group of teachers at my current school began to work collaboratively on an inquiry focusing on how we could assist children to develop research skills. This inquiry was sustained over a number of years and contributed to the professional development of the staff members at our school.

Teacher Collaboration

In October 1990, I began teaching at my school, a small elementary school in an urban, metropolitan area. The school population consists of approximately 180 students from junior kindergarten to grade five. There are five classrooms from grade one to five. The school encourages and fosters a collaborative working relationship among staff members. Conversations about our teaching often take place during lunch hours, before and after school, and during recess breaks. We constantly look to one another in order to communicate about our practices. Our questions, debates, reflections, and suggestions lead to inquiry and continually challenge us to reflect on our practices. These informal inquiry sessions keep changing focus. At times the inquiry is centered on one teacher or classroom, and sometimes the inquiry is centered on the school. This form of "small talk" (Cochran-Smith & Lytle, 1992) serves an important function. Small talk creates and "sustains the interpersonal relationships necessary for the larger project of the joint construction of knowledge" (p. 310).

Our joint work and the focus of our professional development during the 1992–93 school year was a school-based inquiry centered on research skills and how children develop skills as researchers.

The History of Our Collaboration

In order to begin our joint work, our group of six, which consisted of all the primary (grades one to three)/junior (grades four to five) teachers in the school and the special education teacher, began with a question. Our question came from one teacher, who began to discuss the issue of research skills with other colleagues during a "small talk" session. She wondered how we could assist children in acquiring research skills in order to become lifelong learners. This question, which we began to examine in pairs and during informal sessions, became "a shared commitment to a particular agenda that's tied to kids" (Sparks, 1994). The six of us decided in the fall of 1992 that this would become the focus of our professional development. The focus on children's research skills would last for most of the school year and would continue into the summer and the 1993–94 school year.

How do teachers go about assisting students in learning to become critical thinkers? How are these skills learned, and can they be learned by all? These are the questions that we began to examine and attempt to answer as a collaborative group. We came together to examine how we, as individual teachers, were working with the students in our classrooms in the area of research. We asked ourselves what it was that we wanted students to learn while engaged in the research process. We questioned the value of research to lifelong learning, and we wondered what skills our students would need in order to effectively engage in research.

We began with questions that had been initiated by the special education teacher in our school during the 1991–92 school year. The special education teacher was team teaching with three other teachers in the school, and she was working with students who had been deemed learning disabled. She worked on research in the classroom with the teachers and students from grades three to five.

As she worked in these different classrooms, she began to form questions based on her observations. As she shared her thoughts and questions with the teachers she was working with, the questions and network began to grow.

As a result of these questions, the special education teacher met formally with all the primary and junior grade teachers to examine various strategies that could be implemented when teaching students how to successfully research a topic or question. We were all struggling to articulate what we were putting into practice in our classrooms and why we felt that these were appropriate practices. After these few formal meetings, each of us continued to implement various strategies for lifelong learning centered on the area of research skills. We shared the findings of our own teacher research during small talk sessions, but we did not formally meet again as a group until the following year.

Professional Development: A Collaborative Effort

The following year, a collaborative group was formed. Although we had formally met several times in the previous year to examine the issue of research skills, we still had questions about which skills we wanted the students in our school to acquire. It was decided that we would meet regularly throughout the year to discuss how we approached research in our classrooms. Every primary and junior grade teacher, as well as the special education teacher, began to meet each week during our lunch hour. The teacher-librarian also joined us for a number of meetings when her schedule permitted. During this series of weekly meetings held over a period of five months, we questioned, examined, discussed, shared, and reflected together in order to develop a model that would begin in grade one and carry through to grade five. We wanted the focus to be on the process. We wanted this process to have continuity, both in philosophy and practice. We wanted this process to begin in the primary grades and continue through the junior grades. We wanted the students who were leaving our school bound for middle school to understand the role they played in their own learning and to feel confident about their abilities. Although we placed our emphasis on the process, we also realized that the product was important but that it was not to be valued on its own.

We began by sharing what we were doing in our own classrooms. Each of us would come to the meeting and discuss how we were approaching the teaching of research skills in our own classrooms. The special education teacher was able to share what she observed and what was occurring in the various classrooms in which she team taught, as well as any strategies or ideas she had learned from her special education inservice meetings. Each member of the group contributed successes, failures, questions, ideas, strategies, and most important, support, for one another. The group felt at ease discussing both what worked and what did not work. As each person shared, the main ideas and questions were recorded by one member of the group, and a focus and date for our next meeting was set.

Although our meetings were scheduled once a week during our lunch hour, occasionally we would meet twice a week. The number of meetings fluctuated depending on the stage of our questioning and our own individual classroom inquiries. The meeting schedule also considered the time of year and other events occurring at the school. Therefore, around report card writing time, fewer meetings might be scheduled. We also gauged the energy level of the group. Sometimes a scheduled meeting would be canceled due to "overload" (for both professional and personal reasons); and at other times, when energy levels were high, two meetings might be scheduled in one week.

Giroux (1987) believes that teachers must critically examine their own practices and raise serious questions about what and why they are teaching. Each teacher always came to the meetings with questions, comments, observations, strategies, or anecdotes that had been gathered and recorded in his or her own classroom. Each week, the interaction varied, depending on the direction of our comments and questions. What remained constant during these meetings was the willingness to share and the spirit of inquiry. No one ever felt that they had "the answer." Group members would describe classroom scenarios and experiences. As these experiences were shared, feedback was provided in various forms. Further questions were raised, similar experiences were shared, the experience described was further examined, and ways to expand on the experience might be suggested. Our discussions often involved debate as we probed and examined issues.

As well as sharing what was occurring in our own classrooms, we discussed what we had learned by reading the current research in the area we were exploring. Darling-Hammond (1994) believes that "professionalism starts from the proposition that thoughtful and ethical use of knowledge must inform practice" (p. 4). The examination of the research literature provided us with further questions and issues to be examined.

As teachers, we must continually examine our practices and ask critical questions of ourselves. Atwell (1991) states that "one way we do this is by learning from the best research reports and by recognizing that close reading and disciplined debate about what we have read will strengthen, not dilute, our power as thoughtful practitioners" (p. 16).

As the year continued, our group developed a research skills model that we implemented from grades one to five. We began to work through the model with all the primary and junior students in our school. That summer, we continued to meet as a group, and we formalized our philosophy. Over the period of one year at least 70 hours were spent examining the issue of research skills.

Our search and struggle to define learning as a group of professionals led us to examine the issues involved in helping children learn how to research. What we did as a group of teachers was important and necessary. It was initiated and coordinated by us and sustained through our collaboration. During our meetings, we shared our thoughts and beliefs about learning. We discussed different methods and approaches that we could use in our classrooms. We continued to question and refine our model, our philosophy, and our practices during the following year. We continued to monitor the process and discuss what was occurring in our own classrooms, as well as what was written in the research literature.

The Effects of Teacher Collaboration

Four years have passed since those initial few meetings were held during the 1991–92 school year. The majority of our collaborative efforts took place during the 1992–93 school year, but the effects of that collaboration were most visible during the 1993–94 and 1994–95 school years. The students in grades three to five had been exposed to our philosophy and practices for three to four years. The students were moving along a continuum of classroom research that went from large group research in the primary grades to becoming independent researchers by the time they reached the junior grades.

The majority of students were able to discuss the various stages of research, and they understood the research process. Many of the areas that we investigated with our students were taken from the curriculum guidelines written by the board of education in our district.

We began with the large topic and built a common knowledge base for the entire class. From this knowledge base, the students began to focus on personal areas of interest and to brainstorm what they knew about this topic of interest. Duckworth (1987) states that curriculum can suggest ideas to students; it should raise questions and inspire learners to explore these questions. She believes that students build "wonderful ideas" by exploring other wonderful ideas, as well as developing wonderful ideas through questioning. "The right question at the right time can move children to peaks in their thinking that result in significant steps forward and real intellectual excitement" (p. 5). The students were encouraged to develop questions and investigate their questions, using a variety of media. Textbooks were not used. We relied on literature from the school and public library, films, excursions, and information from a variety of sources. The sources from which the students gathered information continued to grow as the students began to realize the wide range of possibilities. The students were taught how to make "jot notes" based on information that they gathered, and they learned to categorize and sort these notes. One student wrote in a self-evaluation, "I am quite good at sorting jots into categories. It's a thing that you have to think a lot about. But sometimes there's one jot that goes with two categories. But the fun thing about it is it's like being a detective."

Once the students had categorized and organized their information, they presented final products. Their products involved writing and often oral presentation. The writing included formal reports, fictional stories containing the relevant information to be presented, and diaries. The oral presentations took the form of drama, formal reports, and videos. Again, just as the students learned that the possibilities for gathering information were endless, they also learned that they could present informa-

tion in various ways. The students were helping design and structure the curriculum. Harste (1993) states that:

> Curriculum is not a course to be run. Rather, curriculum is a meaning-making potential where knowledge is created, acted upon, and recreated at the point of experience. It provides opportunities for both teachers and students to experience themselves as learners, engaged together in inquiry in order to create, critique, and transcend their present realities. (p. 5)

Implications of Our Collaboration

Our students inquire. They are curious, and they understand the importance of this curiosity and their own questions. They are now able to articulate the research process. They know how to access information in order to examine the issues surrounding their questions, and they have learned that research usually leads to further inquiry.

As well as articulating the research process for ourselves and our students, we also articulated our practices and expectations to the parents in our school community. Through the use of self-evaluations, newsletters, report card comments, parent-teacher meetings, and open houses, the students' parents were aware of our beliefs and philosophy. They were able to assist their children in becoming lifelong learners by working in partnership with the school. As one parent responded on a self-evaluation, "My daughter presented her research to me at home and I agree that she put a lot of hard work and enthusiasm into her research. I was impressed by the organization of the presentation which comes from the way you guided them through the process."

The benefits of our collaboration were evident as we worked with our students in the classroom. As a junior classroom teacher (grades three to four), I worked with the students who had been exposed to the model since grade one. These students were comfortable with the steps that we had developed, and they viewed themselves as competent, independent researchers.

Developing a research skills model was the focus of our group inquiry. Collaboration surrounding any number of issues could have been pursued. The success of both our model and our collaboration was because of the group's ability to come together and share in the leadership as we developed curriculum. How can collaborative cultures be encouraged and maintained in schools? What factors contribute to the shared leadership that Fullan (1994) is calling for?

Collaborative Cultures: Where Do We Go From Here?

Nias, Southward, and Yeomans (1989) discuss the characteristics of collaborative cultures. The following characteristics were found where such cultures existed:

1. Collaboration was found in all aspects of school life.

2. Failure and uncertainty are shared, discussed, and examined in order to receive help, support, and insight.

3. There was broad agreement on educational values.

4. Members who collaborate tolerate disagreement; this disagreement can be frequent as teachers continually question and examine, and common purposes are shared and developed over time

5. The total person counts in collaborative cultures; interdependence is valued and diversity is valued.

I believe that our group worked as a collaborative culture. Each of these characteristics applies to our group as we worked together over time. Rather than working in isolation, we "cracked the walls of privatism" (Fullan & Hargreaves, 1991, p. 6) in order to "work together, learn from each other, and improve" our "expertise as a community" (Fullan & Hargreaves, 1991, p. 1). Our group initiative greatly benefited each member of the group as well as the students in our school. Although this collaboration had many positive effects, a number of questions still remain and must be examined.

Our collaborative group effort stemmed from our own interests and inquiry. We each voluntarily decided to meet during our own time because time was not made available for us during the school day. Time has been identified as one of the key factors in maintaining a collaborative culture (Darling-Hammond, 1994; Fullan, 1993). If teachers are to work together to develop professionally, where will this time come from? Will this initiative be supported by both administration and the community? As well as setting aside time for teachers to meet, members of the group need opportunities to "work through complicated issues over time, then ideas have a chance to incubate and develop, trust builds in the group, and participants feel comfortable raising sensitive issues and risking self-revelation" (Cochran-Smith & Lytle, 1992, p. 306). Our group correctly made use of both of the concepts of time.

Will our collaboration continue over the next few years? Changes to our staff occurred during the 1994–1995 school year. Two of the teachers in our group were no longer teaching at the school. The special education teacher whose original questions helped to form our collaborative group transferred to a new school. Another teacher took a year off to spend time with her infant son and complete her graduate work. Despite these changes, our collaboration continued during this year. As part of her graduate work, the teacher who took a year

off returned and led group sessions on spelling. These sessions involved most of our original group, as well as some new staff members. We agreed to meet to discuss the issue of spelling during lunch hour sessions. We have questions surrounding this aspect of the curriculum and hope to be able to develop a school wide philosophy in the area of spelling, just as we did with research skills. (Chapter 7 describes the group spelling sessions in detail.)

We agreed as a staff in September that our focus for the year would be on literacy across the grades. Our professional development for the 1994–95 school year was supported by our administration. To provide the teachers on staff with time to meet regularly, our principal freed up all of the teachers on staff, twice a week, for two half-hour periods. She accomplished this by leading a schoolwide assembly during these times. This solution is due in part to our small school population.

By leading schoolwide assemblies, the principal enabled the whole staff to meet during school hours, which does not impinge on personal time. It also ensures that all staff members will be present at the meetings because group collaboration has become a valued aspect of the school culture. Now each teacher in the school is able to participate in collaborative professional development. This opportunity has allowed staff members to develop curriculum, set policy, and make administrative decisions as a school team. Each teacher shares equally in responsibility and in decision making. Teachers who have been at the school for a number of years, as well as those who recently joined the staff, feel that the time made available to meet is important. The meetings will continue in the following year.

Until there is systematic change and collaborative cultures are valued and supported by school administrations, large-scale change is not possible. However, change begins with individual teachers. Fullan (1994) states that

> individual and small group action will turn out to be a more powerful strategy than relying on institutional action. As individual teachers and small groups of teachers begin to work in their own schools, external and internal forces eventually must connect if there is to be institutional progress. (p. 251)

This new professionalism will focus on teacher expertise and knowledge, coupled with collaborative efforts among teams of teachers, schools, and the community. We need to critically examine our teaching practices and the implications of these practices on students. We need to explore the question of how to use time and expertise in order to create and sustain these workplace cultures to further develop teaching.

REFERENCES

Atwell, N. (1991). *Side by side: Essays on teaching to learn.* Portsmouth, NH: Heinemann.

Cochran-Smith, M., & Lytle, S. (1992). Communities for Teacher Research: Fringe or Forefront? *American Journal of Education, 100,* 298–322.

Darling-Hammond, L. (1994). *Professional development schools: Schools for developing a profession.* New York: Teachers College Press.

Duckworth, E. (1987). *"The having of wonderful ideas" and other essays: Teaching and learning.* New York: Teachers College Press.

Fullan, M. (1993). *Change forces: Probing the depths of educational reform.* New York: Falmer Press.

Fullan, M. (1994). Teacher leadership: A failure to conceptualize. In Walling, Donovan R. (Ed.), *Teachers as leaders: Perspectives on the professional development of teachers* (pp. 241-253). Bloomington, IN: Phi Delta Kappa Educational Foundation.

Fullan, M., & Hargreaves, A. (1991). *What's worth fighting for? Working together for your school.* Andover, MA: The Regional Laboratory for Educational Improvement of the Northeast and Islands.

Giroux, H.A. (1987). Critical literacy and student experience: Donald Graves' approach to literacy. *Language Arts, 64,* 175–181.

Harste, J.C. (1993). Inquiry-based instruction. *Primary Voices, K–6, 1,* 2–5.

Nias, J., Southward, G., & Yeomans, R. (1989). *Staff relationships in the primary school.* London: Cassell Educational Limited.

Sparks, D. (1994). *Dennis Sparks interviews Judith Warren Little on professional development in school reform.* Oxford, OH: National Staff Development Council.

CHAPTER 9

Wild Dreams and Sober Cautions: The Future of Teacher Research

Marian M. Mohr

Through her book Working Together *(with Marion MacLean) and her journal articles and presentations at conferences, Mohr has been a significant contributor to current thinking about the potentials and the complexities of teacher research. She has taught at the secondary and postsecondary level and is currently conducting research with The Teacher-Researcher Project, a federally funded program in Fairfax County, Virginia, USA.*

■ I am a worrier. I want to be prepared when the sun burns out. When people say, "You're going to love this," I feel an existential dread and immediately try to figure out how to keep from hurting their feelings. I fear predicting too rosy a future, acting on too little data or too shallow an analysis, or relying on too much hope and too high a regard for people's ability to change.

These worries and fears are useful to me as a teacher researcher in the classroom. I know of no way to teach without too much hope and too high a regard for people's ability to change. I know of no way to research without caution and doubt, without the curiosity to start over, to rethink and reflect, steeling

myself to observe and record with honesty. In my worried mind, predictions for the future of teacher research are both hopeful and cautious. My first prediction is my most confident.

Teachers at all grade levels and in all different kinds of teaching situations will be conducting research and presenting their ideas to their colleagues.

At the 1995 International Conference on Teacher Research I met teacher researchers from all over the world. At the 1995 American Educational Research Association meeting I heard university teachers discuss research they were conducting on their own practice and report on school-university collaboration that, for the first time, sounded to me like real collaboration. Their reports credited all participants as authors, and as they had taught and researched, together they presented their findings. In my own community I have worked with English as a second language, community college, adult education, and K–12 public school teachers, all of whom are teaching as a research process. Whether the process is called teacher research, action research, or teacher-led inquiry, it has a found a place in the profession and it does not seem to be disappearing.

The prospect that teacher research will fade is sobering, but also possible. I entered the field 15 years ago through an interest in writing research; I now hear the teaching of writing process referred to as a "fad." In a recent issue of an educational tabloid, an article proclaimed that teachers of writing process have abandoned thinking in favor of feeling and expression. The article was written as an alarm; it quoted without context and generalized without evidence. It reminded me of the way educational decisions are often made—not based on careful observation and not mindful of biases and assumptions, but pushing ahead in a desperate move to change something or to accuse someone of failing or being out of date.

What if teacher research comes to be viewed as a fad? What if support disappears for teachers to conduct and present their research? These questions raise doubts about my prediction, but what if teacher researchers look at new educational directions and add them to their list of possible research subjects? Because teacher research is a way of teaching as well as a way of gathering information, it is not tied to what is new. Teacher researchers value the work of other researchers and respect the requirements of their school system, but their work is internally motivated, based on their day-to-day interactions with students.

Teacher research represents something entirely different from the usual staff development efforts to introduce a curriculum or method change. It is the opposite of the what-to-do-on-Monday-morning or 45-minutes-after-school inservice approach to teaching. A teacher research report does not resemble a "What Works" pamphlet or a "List of Proven Strategies." It is a different way of looking at teaching altogether, which leads to a second prediction.

Teacher-researchers will contribute to new definitions of what it means to teach.

I may be going too far on this point, probably because these ideas about teaching are related to the research I am doing on what happens in the classrooms of teacher researchers. I am in a hopeful phase.

What does this new definition look like? Teacher researchers see their work as a process of asking questions and exploring, with their students, possible answers to those questions. They step back to observe occasionally, instead of immediately acting to solve, instruct, correct, or praise. They are the adult contributors to the learning in their classrooms. Rather than being master teachers, they are master students. They use their knowledge and experience to create with their students a repertoire of ways of learning. Their classroom curriculum is based on their district and school curriculum, but is extended to include the knowledge and learning experience their students bring with them.

Teacher researchers learn in front of their students, demonstrating and discussing the processes that a researcher—a learner—goes through. Their students watch this learner at work and see not only what there is to learn, but ways to learn it. The students discuss how they learn and talk with one another about learning strategies. They see their mistakes as data about learning, useful to them and their teachers.

The definition of teaching that results from this description not only changes our ideas about what teaching is, but also implies the revamping of ideas about how teachers learn to teach and ideas about staff development and preservice training. I do not yet see the effect of teacher research on most professional development programs. Inservice programs that I attend, even those enlightened by workshop approaches, nei-

ther acknowledge nor respect the expertise of the teachers in the room. There are whole meetings and conferences about teaching at which no or few K–12 teachers are present. Such meetings operate in a repair and improvement mode—whatever teachers are doing is inadequate and unreasonable. When their model of professional development is used on a group of teachers, often at the end of a school day or in an evening course, it is not surprising that the teachers find many ways to reject what is offered and defend themselves against what they perceive as attack.

It is also not surprising that when these teachers ignore the insults offered by the situation and decide to try the new methods, they do so with respect for their own classroom decision making, their own knowledge of classroom context, and their own strengths as teachers. When teachers do adapt and extend new methods they are sometimes criticized for not "doing it right" or not being true to the model. I realize that I am moving beyond caution to gloom, but it has always astounded and depressed me to discover, even in the presence of my obvious eagerness to learn to be a better teacher, how little my own learning and experience, and those of my teaching colleagues, are valued by those who want me to change.

Teacher research is a do-it-yourself-with-the-help-of-colleagues model of teacher learning. At the heart of the professionalism that teacher research offers is respect for teacher knowledge—not teacher folklore or faculty lounge laments, but knowledge as it is acquired by research. The value of this knowledge leads to a third prediction.

Teacher research will contribute to the knowledge base of the profession, and teacher researchers will participate as equal partners in the discourse of the profession.

Leona Bernard, Mary Ann Gianotti, Catherine Keating, Christina Konjevic, Maria Kowal, Ann Maher, Connie Mayer, Tamara Moscoe, Ewa Orzechowska, Anna Smieja, and Larry Swartz, and Gordon Wells (1994) at the Ontario Institute for Studies in Education have written eloquently about the ways that teacher research changes teachers and schools from within. I agree that change from within is both fundamental and profound, and is the only way to achieve lasting reform in education. Ignorance of this principle of change has caused many reforms to founder.

Changes within classrooms and schools, however, may not affect the educational community at large. Whenever I have tried to limit my teaching and research to my own classroom, plans and pronouncements from the larger educational community have intruded. Teaching and teacher research are not done independently of the profession. Teacher research is not a move out of teaching, but is a move toward a more responsible role in the school system and a new relationship with colleagues at all levels.

In my imagination, an understanding of the need for change in these educational relationships takes the form of a large book. It's title would be something like *Research and Practice in the Language Arts for the 1990's: A Handbook for Educators*. The table of contents is filled with articles written by various leaders in our profession. In the beginning of the book, the articles about theory are all written by people who have university affiliations after their names. Perhaps that is not so surprising. After all, theory is still regarded as an "ivory tower" occupation in some educational circles. In the next group of articles labeled "Research," the authors have university affiliations as well. Finally, in the sections of the book that are about practice—that is, teaching—again, the authors are labeled with universities.

I have read books like this and learned from their contents. I respect the work of many individuals with university affiliations, but I want to consider the message this book would send. Not only does it say that theory and research belong to colleges and universities, but also that practices based on these theories and research must be interpreted and designed for K–12 teachers by college and university professors.

The problem becomes more complex when we consider that the book would be purchased as a text for courses that teach teachers how to teach. People entering teaching would be taught that they will not be the knowledge makers of their profession, that even the mentor teachers they will come to know—who will help them enormously in their efforts to learn how to teach—do not contribute to the knowledge base of teaching.

Who else buys the book? Staff development directors and curriculum specialists buy it to make sure their teachers are up to date, checking their curriculum against the latest research and theory and looking for people to give inservice presentations to teachers about how to improve their teaching. Once more the message goes out.

My hopeful prediction is different. In the future, K–12 teachers will contribute articles in all categories to such a book. Article bibliographies will indicate references to works by K–12 teachers. Those who edit and publish such books will not consider them comprehensive without theory, research, and practice by K–12 teachers. The university researchers will not disappear, but they will share knowledge building with their K–12 colleagues. A different message will go out to both preservice and inservice teachers—the message that students and teachers, working together, each have something to offer in the attempt to understand what goes on in schools.

My fourth and final prediction stems from this book of the future, so it is the prediction about which I am the least sure.

Teacher research, by its rethinking of the basic questions of education, will reshape the understanding of how children learn and will transform our schools into learning communities.

An immediate caution: "learning community" is a term that makes me uneasy. It sounds so idealistic, and is more inclusive than the team often favored by educational administrators. The truth is that I am not sure it is possible to create a learning community.

I worry that we will not be able to move toward a community of learners because we have rejected the idea of community and have grown accustomed to seeing ourselves as various labeled groups with nothing in common to build on. I worry about the United States's attitude toward its children as well as its teachers. I worry that families in our communities see schools as frightening, rather than helpful or professional. I worry that teacher research will not be available and accepted in time to help us understand and teach the students who are new to our classrooms, whose languages and cultures we do not always know or understand.

I worry that as college teachers join with K–12 teacher researchers to critically examine their own practice and the learning of their students, they will be regarded as doing less important work because they study the teaching of their discipline, in addition to elements of the discipline itself. I worry that they will not earn tenure or promotions because of their identification with K-12 teacher researchers.

When my worries start to multiply, as a teacher researcher I know to return to reflection and research, to try to see the pattern in the data.

Recently I met with a small group of teacher researchers in Winchester, Virginia. We had begun working on our research in October; it was now April. The group had a shared background in language arts. One group member was a third-year teacher who had been a student of some of the other teachers in the group. Another member, now an assistant principal after 20 years in the classroom, was looking for ways to bring teacher evaluation together with the realities of teaching as she knew it. The ten of us sat around a table as we each reported on our research from the year's work.

The assistant superintendent had come to listen. She had helped convince the principals of the two high schools where the teachers taught that some school funding should support us in our work, and now she was curious about our findings. As a group, we had also written a code of ethics and standards for conducting teacher research in the district.

It was 7:30 p.m. when we finished, and I was in awe of what I had heard. The conversation was full of insights and findings, of newly forged research relationships with students, and of renewed confidence and determination. One teacher talked about the difficulty of asking the right questions in the right way at the right time. Several teachers agreed that it was important that their students know that teachers have an interest in how they learn. One teacher said, "It makes you take what they have to say more seriously." Most of the talk was about teaching—specific teaching ideas, how they worked in the classroom, and what the teachers planned to try next. Suddenly I thought, "This *is* one—this is a community of learners! They exists! I thought of other teacher-research groups and their similar characteristics. Maybe teacher researchers, as a source of knowledge of what constitutes a learning community, can teach others and demonstrate what a learning community means.

Why do I assume that teacher research—so hard to do, so hard to explain—is so valuable? Because my worries are so deep. The public education system staggers under the pressure of many demands and may not recognize in teacher researchers the knowledge and strength needed to teach children. As researchers, we accept the struggle and the responsibility of learning; as teachers, we know that to learn is to hope.

Author's Note: An earlier version of this essay was delivered at the International Reading Association's 40th Annual Convention in Anaheim, California, USA, May 1995.

REFERENCE

Wells, G. , Bernard, L., Gianotti, M., Keating, C., Konjevic, C., Kowal, M., Maher, A., Mayer, C., Moscoe, T., Orzechowska, E., Smieja, A., and Swartz, L. (1994). *Changing schools from within: Creating communities of inquiry*. Toronto: Ontario Institute for Studies in Education Press.

Author Index

S

Sandburg, C., 12, 35
Santa, C.M., 1
Savignon, S., 53, 62, 63
Schaafsma, D., 90
Schon, D.A., 37, 50
Scott-Dunne, D., 101, 107
Shechter, M., 99, 102
Sherlock, P., 52, 63
Shor, I., 81, 90
Short, K.G., 1
Siegel, M.G., 10, 34
Simmons, R., 48, 50
Smieja, A., 9, 120, 123
Smith, F., 66, 80
Smith, K., 1
Smucker, B., 42, 50
Snow, M., 24
Southward, G., 114, 116
Sparks, D., 105, 108, 109, 116
Spradley, J.P., 11, 34
St. Pierre-Hirtle, J., 2, 81
Strasser, T., 12, 35
Strickland, D.S., 100, 105, 107
Swartz, L., 9, 60, 64, 120, 123

T

Taylor, T., 16, 35
Teacher as Researcher Ad Hoc
    Committee, 1
Todnem, G.R., 37, 49, 50, 60, 63
Twain, M., 16, 35

V

Voss, M.M., 27, 34
Vygotsky, L.S., 6, 7, 9, 68-69, 80

W

Warren Little, J., 116
Weaver, C., 24, 34
Wells, G., 8, 9, 60, 64, 99, 104, 107,
    120, 123
Wertsch, J.V., 67, 68, 80
White, R., 30, 35
Wilkinson, A., 63, 64
Williams, D.D., 10, 11
Woodward, V.A., 4, 7, 9, 27, 31, 34

Y

Yashinsky, D., 51, 59, 64
Yeomans, R., 114, 116

Z

Zukav, G., 82, 90

Subject Index

Note: An "f" following a page number indicates that the reference may be found in a figure; a "t" indicates that it may be found in a table.

A

ABDUCTIVE ENVIRONMENTS, 7
ACTION: reflection on, 37
ACTION RESEARCH, 49, 60
ACTIVE LISTENING, 75
AMERICAN EDUCATIONAL RESEARCH ASSOCIATION, 117
ANANSI STORIES, 51–52, 54–59
ANECDOTES, 8
AUDIOTAPES, 38–39
AUTHORS: link with teacher community, 100–101

B

BANKING CONCEPT OF EDUCATION, 86
BOOKKEEPERS: journals as, 25–26

C

CHEERLEADING, 16–22
CHILDREN: attitude toward, 121; as informants, 27; interview responses, 96–98
CHILDREN'S LITERATURE REFERENCES, 34–35, 50, 64
CLASSROOM COMMUNITY, 92–93; link with teacher community, 95–98; link with university research community, 101–102

CLASSROOM INQUIRY, 105
CLASSROOM TALK AND TEXTS: learning from, 3–9
CLASSROOMS: reflecting, 36–50
CLOSE READING, 28
COLLABORATION: with communities, 104–106; communities of inquiry project, 91–92; professional development groups, 110–112; teacher, 108–109, 112–113
COLLABORATIVE CULTURES, 114–116; characteristics of, 114
COLLABORATIVE INQUIRY PROJECT, 108–116; collaborative groups, 110–112; history, 109–110; implications, 113–114
COLLABORATIVE LEARNING: for students, 85–86; for teachers, 84–85
COLLABORATIVE RESEARCH AND REFLECTION: potentials for change and professionalism, 8
COLLABORATIVE TECHNOLOGY PROJECT, 81; beginnings, 81–83; Christmas book publication, 84; developing, 83–84; students, 85–86; teachers, 84–85; what we learned, 90
COMMUNICATION: continuing conversations, 2; conversations in science classrooms, 8; learning through discourse, 8–9; mediation of learning by, 5–6; modes of discourse, 94–95, 102–104
COMMUNITIES: being part of, 60–61; collaboration with, 104–106; learning, 5

COMMUNITIES OF INQUIRY PROJECT, 91–93; children's interview responses, 96–98; classroom community, 92–93; communities, 92–94; community of educators, 94; community of researchers and writers, 93–94; e-mail, 95; link between author and teacher communities, 100–101; link between classroom and teacher communities, 95–98; link between classroom and university research communities, 101–102; link between teacher group and university research communities, 98–100; looking ahead, 102–106; minutes of teacher meetings, 94; modes of discourse, 94–95; monthly meetings, 94; summaries of literature, 95; teacher community, 93; teacher interviews, 105–106; transcripts of interviews, 95; university research community, 93

COMPLEX SYSTEMS: learning communities, 5

COMPUTER TECHNOLOGY: benefits and challenges, 86–88; collaborative technology project, 81–86, 90

CONCEPTS: scientific, 68–69; spontaneous, 68

CONSTRUCTIVISM, 67–69

CONVERSATIONS: continuing, 2; in science classrooms, 8

CULTURES: collaborative, 114–116

CURRICULUM, 113

D

DISCOURSE: learning through, 8–9; mediation of learning by, 5–6; modes of, 94–95, 102–104

E

EDUCATION: banking concept of, 86

EDUCATORS: community of, 94

ELABORATION, 54–56

ELEMENTARY GEOMETRY: language experience approach to, 65–80

ELEMENTARY SCHOOL: collaborative inquiry project, 108–116

E-MAIL, 95; sample correspondences, 98–102; uses, 98–100

ENVIRONMENTS: abductive, 7

F–H

FACE-TO-FACE PROMOTIVE INTERACTION, 85

FIRST PERSON: storytelling in, 57–58

FLUENCY: lack of, 52–54

GEOMETRY: language experience approach to, 65–80

GUTKNECHT, PAT, 83

HIGH SCHOOL STUDENTS: collaborative technology project, 81–86, 90

I

INQUIRY: classroom, 105; collaborative inquiry project, 108–116; communities of inquiry project, 91–107; reflective, 7–8; shared, 4–8; storytelling as, 60

INTERACTION: face-to-face promotive, 85

INTERNATIONAL CONFERENCE ON TEACHER RESEARCH 1995, 117

INTERVIEWS: with children, 70, 77–78, 96–98; with teachers, 69–70, 105–106; transcripts of, 95

ISAKSON, MARNÉ: dialogue about teacher journals, 11–33

J–K

JOURNALS, 33; effects on teaching practice, 11; mentor/friend role of, 26; power of, 15; rules for deciding what to write, 14; teacher, 10–35; Think Books, 39–43; use of, 16, 17*f*, 18

KID WATCHING, 10, 26

L

LANGUAGE: indications of skill, 52–54; and learning, 65–66; as ultimate tool, 68

LANGUAGE EXPERIENCE APPROACH TO ELEMENTARY GEOMETRY, 65–80; classroom observations, 70–77; conclusion, 78–80; final children's interview, 77–78; findings, 69–78; first children's interview, 70; first lesson, 70–76; first teacher interview, 69–70; lesson three, 76–77; lesson two, 76; transcripts, 71–75

LEARNERS: peer-learners, 20–21; teachers as, 21–22, 29

LEARNING: from classroom talk and texts, 3–9; collaborative, 84–86; language and, 65–66; mediation by discourse, 5–6; reflective inquiry fuel, 7–8; reliving, 9; as shared inquiry, 4–8; as social and transactional, 4–5; stories, 51–64; student-directed, 60; through discourse, 8–9

LEARNING COMMUNITIES: complex systems, 5; terminology, 121

LEARNING CONVERSATIONS: in science classrooms, 8

LEARNING LOGS: polylogs, 3, 6; Think Books, 39–43. *see also* Journals

LIBERAL ARTS: tools of, 60

LISTENING: active, 75

LISTENING HELPERS, 27–28

LITERACY EVENTS, 12

LITERATURE: references, 34–35, 50, 64; summaries of, 95

M

MANAGEMENT: total quality management (TQM) training, 89

MATHEMATICS: language experience approach to elementary geometry, 65–80

MEETINGS: minutes of, 94; monthly, 94

MINUTES OF TEACHER MEETINGS, 94

MODES OF DISCOURSE, 94–95; revising, 102–104

MONTHLY MEETINGS, 94

N

NOTEBOOKS: polylogs, 3, 6; Think Books, 39–43. *see also* Journals

NOTES: looking at, 14; pondering, 14; recording, 14; taking, 13

O

OBSERVATIONS, 12

OBSERVER COMMENTS, 12

ORAL REFLECTION: whole class, 44–47

OVERLOAD, 111

P

PEER-LEARNERS, 20–21

POLYLOGS, 3, 6

PORTFOLIOS, 6, 87

PROFESSIONAL DEVELOPMENT: collaborative groups, 110–112; collaborative inquiry project, 108–116

PROFESSIONAL PRACTICE, 24

PROFESSIONALISM, 8, 116

PROMOTIVE INTERACTION: face-to-face, 85

PROXIMAL DEVELOPMENT: zone of, 69

PSYCHOLOGICAL TOOLS, 68

Q–R

QUALITY MANAGEMENT: total quality management (TQM) training, 89

READING: close, 28; transactional theory of, 31

REFLECTING CLASSROOMS, 36–50

REFLECTION, 12; about reflection, 48–49; on action, 37; collaborative, 8; collaborative technology project, 81–86, 90; on the run, 88–90; safe environments for, 45; small group, 47–48; student, 37–48; teacher, 31, 36–37; technology and, 81–90; whole class oral, 44–47

REFLECTIVE INQUIRY, 7–8

REPORTS: teacher research, 118

RESEARCH: action, 60; collaborative, 8; continuing conversation, 2; modes of discourse for, 94–95, 102–104; teacher, 117–123; university community, 93, 98–102

RESEARCH AND PRACTICE IN THE LANGUAGE ARTS FOR THE 1990'S: A HANDBOOK FOR EDUCATORS, 120

RESEARCHERS: community of, 93–94; teachers, 1–2, 60–61, 118–121

S

SCIENCE CLASSROOMS: learning conversations in, 8

SCIENTIFIC CONCEPTS, 68–69

SELF-DISCOVERY, 33

SELF-EVALUATIONS: written, 43–44

SELF-TALK, 18

SERVICE TO STUDENTS: how journals enhance, 25–29

SHARED INQUIRY: teaching and learning as, 4–8

SMALL GROUP REFLECTION, 47–48

SMALL TALK, 109

SOCIOCULTURAL THEORY, 67–69

SPELLING: communities of inquiry project, 91–107; researchers and writers about, 93–94

SPONTANEOUS CONCEPTS, 68

STAFF DEVELOPMENT PROGRAMS: essential features, 105

STORIES: Anansi, 51–52; process of learning, 51–64; real interpretation of, 60; visualizing, 58–60

STORYTELLING: in first person, 57–58; as inquiry, 60; role for students, 62; student, 51–64; understanding, 62–63; visualizing, 58–60; why bother with, 62

STUDENT PORTFOLIOS: excerpts, 87

STUDENT REFLECTION, 37–48; with audiotapes and videotapes, 38–39; with Think Books, 39–43; what students say, 48; written self-evaluations, 43–44

STUDENT STORYTELLING, 51–64; data collection, 52; elaboration, 54–56; examples, 54–58; false starts, 52–54; in first person, 57–58

STUDENT–DIRECTED LEARNING, 60

STUDENTS: collaborative learning for, 85–86; collaborative technology project, 81–86; how journals enhance service to, 25–29; role of storytelling for, 62

SUMMARIES OF LITERATURE, 95

SYSTEMS: complex, 5

T

TALK: classroom, 3–9; small, 109

TEACHER COLLABORATION, 108–109; effects of, 112–113

TEACHER COMMUNITIES, 93; link with authors, 100–101; link with classroom communities, 95–98; link with university research communities, 98–100

TEACHER INTERVIEWS, 69–70, 105–106

TEACHER JOURNALS, 10–35; bookkeeper role, 25–26; cheerleading role, 16–22; contrasting, 13, 13t; dialogue about, 11–33; excerpts, 11–12, 15–16, 18–19, 22–25, 27–28, 30–31; getting started, 29–30; how they enhance service to students, 25–29; how they facilitate thinking about teaching, 22–25; how they pay off, 30–31; peer-learner role, 20–21; rules for deciding what to write, 14; suggested approach for, 33; why tell about, 31–33

TEACHER MEETINGS: minutes of, 94

TEACHER REFLECTION, 31, 36–37

TEACHER RESEARCH: future of, 117–123; looking ahead, 102; modes of discourse for, 91–107; predictions for, 117–123; reports, 118

TEACHERS: attitude toward, 121; collaborative learning for, 84–85; how journals help maintain self as, 16–22; as learners, 21–22, 29; learning, 29; as researchers, 1–2, 60–61, 118–121

TEACHING: definition of, 118–120; how journals facilitate thinking about, 22–25; reflective inquiry fuel, 7–8; as shared inquiry, 4–8; ways to use journal writing to facilitate, 16, 17f

TECHNICAL TOOLS, 68

TECHNOLOGY: collaborative technology project, 81–86, 90; computer, 86–88; and reflection, 81–90

TEXTS: classroom, 3–9

THINK BOOKS, 39–43, 48; excerpts, 40–42

THINKING ABOUT TEACHING: how journals facilitate, 22–25

TOOLS: of arts, 60; role played by, 68

TOTAL QUALITY MANAGEMENT (TQM) TRAINING, 89

TQM TRAINING. see Total quality management training

TRANSACTIONAL THEORY OF READING, 31

TRANSCRIPTS: of interviews, 95; of language experience approach to elementary geometry, 71–75

U–V

UNIVERSITY RESEARCH COMMUNITY, 93; link with classroom community, 101–102; link with teacher groups, 98–100

VIDEOTAPES, 38–39

VISUAL NOVEL STUDIES, 43–44

VISUALIZING STORIES, 58–60

VYGOTSKY, L.S.: sociocultural theory, 67–68; theory on role played by tools, 68

W

WHOLE CLASS ORAL REFLECTION, 44–47

WILLIAMS, DAVID: dialogue about teacher journals, 11–33

WRITERS COMMUNITY, 93–94; link with teacher community, 100–101

WRITING: journal, 11, 14, 16, 17f

WRITTEN SELF-EVALUATIONS, 43–44; format for, 43; samples, 44

Z

ZONE OF PROXIMAL DEVELOPMENT, 69